TRIBHUVAI
for the **TRIB**

(A guide to your solutions...)

MORARI BAPU

BlueRose ONE.com
Stories Matter

First Published in July 2023

ISBN: 978-93-5741-585-9

BLUEROSE PUBLISHERS
www.BlueRoseONE.com
info@bluerosepublishers.com
+91 8882 898 898

Contributor:
Chitrakutdham Trust

Cover Design:
Muskan Sachdeva

Typographic Design:
Pooja Sharma

Distributed by: BlueRose, Amazon, Flipkart

|| श्री ||

"कोरोना की भारती" - तनोगाथाः श्री
कोरोना काल अर्थ्यप बरथी दिन में
सुंदर कोशिश जो "एरुगा काल" रही
इसमें जो कोशिश हुई सही "हिम्मत को
सही। कुछ संबंध हुआ जो गुंथन्द
लोगों जा रहा है। उसकी विशेष प्रेरणा है
कामकाज सर्मिंग अधिकार को जो प्रारंभिक
प्रेरणा लिया है। जो अमूल्य है। संद्धारे!
यह सहायतसंच सबके जीवन में
संवादी सूर प्रदर करें एम प्रभु प्रार्थना।
यह सत्सूत्र- सर्वसूत्र कल्याण
जो जन आचरण हो- जो हो रहा है
कोरोना काल में यह एक पंचाशित
लेखराव रा। यह जनरल प्रथद है।
सबके जीवन में प्रेरणा भरे तो
दन्य! दन्य!! प्रभु मेरी अंतर प्रेरणा
और प्रभु प्रार्थना। रन युग्मिनूष रात्रा

12·3·2023

II राम II

"कोरोना काल" में कैलास स्थिति त्रिभुवन वट की छाया में झूले पर बैठ कर जो "करुणा काल" रहा उसमें "जो बोले सो हरि कथा" शीर्षक पर कुछ संवाद हुआ वो ग्रन्थस्थ होने जा रहा है, उसकी विशेष प्रसन्नता है!

व्यास पीठ समर्पिता अक्रिता ने जो प्रसादिक प्रयास किया है, वो अमूल्य है! साधु वाद!

ये भगवत संवाद सबके जीवन में संवादी सुर प्रगट करे, ऐसे प्रभु प्रार्थना. ये स्वसुख-सर्वसुख बन जाए, ये अति आवश्यक था-जो हो रहा है.

कोरोना काल में ये एक विचारक वैक्सीन थी!

ये त्रिभुवन प्रसाद हैं.

सबके जीवन को प्रसन्नता से भर दे.

धन्य! धन्या!! पुन: मेरी अति प्रसन्नता और प्रभु प्रार्थना!

राम सुमिरन के साथ।

बापू

साइन (मोरारी दास बापू)

12.03.23

About Morari Bapu

Morari Bapu was born in a Margi Sadhu family on the auspicious day of Maha Shivratri on 2nd March 1946, at his ancestral house adjacent to the Ram ji Temple in a small village named Talgajarda of Mahuva in the district of Bhavnagar, Gujarat in India.

As a child, Tribhuvandas Bapu, grandfather and Sadaguru of Morari Bapu, taught him the deeper meanings of Goswami Tulsidas' Ram Charita Manas and initiated him on to the path of recitation of the sacred text i.e. narration of Katha. Bapu used to learn 5 couplets daily from his grandfather and recite these quadrupeds and stanzas from the Ramayana whilst walking to and from school, and thus began his journey of memorizing and oration.

By the age of 12, Bapu had already memorized the entire Ramayana, and at the tender age of 14 years, he started reciting Ram Katha. Initially, he sat under a Banyan tree of his village and recited verses from the Ram Charita Manas to three shepherds, and later at the Ramji Temple in his village Talgajarda, and then the closest town of Mahuva.

Every Ram Katha has a different subject which is announced on the first day of Katha and the chosen Chaupai (quadruped) is elaborated upon during the nine days. Bapu's first 9-day Katha outside of Mahuva was in 1965-66 near Amreli, and his first overseas Katha was held in Nairobi, Kenya in 1976. In his journey of over 60 years of reciting over 900 Kathas, Bapu has travelled across India and the world taking with him the central message of 'Truth, Love and Compassion'.

Bapu does not charge any fees for reciting Ram Katha. Bapu's Kathas are purely non-commercial and free for all, with no restrictions of age, gender, caste, creed, or financial status. Each Katha is accompanied with free vegetarian meals for all who wish to come and partake, whether or not they are listening to the discourse.

Bapu endeavours to reach the "last-man" by actively contributing to various social causes based upon need of the hour. For example, he was the first to have given a Katha to prostitutes, scheduled caste communities and transgenders.

Morari Bapu also brings much delight to the rich and poor alike by accepting Bhiksha (food as alms) from them irrespective of their belief, race, religion, or social strata. Bapu has supported many social and environmental causes calling for the protection of trees, forests, animals, clean air, and the water bodies. He has also raised funds and sent relief to areas devastated by natural calamities, as well as for medical causes like cancer and emergencies like Covid-19 pandemic.

Foreword

For a world that was bewildered by the new disease called Covid-19 in March 2020, Lockdown came as another shocking novelty. Never had humans been so restricted by ailment and circumstance, rather by the consequences of their own making.

Not since the Spanish Flu or Black Death in Europe had the world seen affliction at such a wide scale. Perhaps, this was the first in history if one were to go only by the scope of its spread.

Baffled and intimidated, a ray of hope rose from a Kutiya (cottage) in a remote village in India's state of Gujarat. These were words of solace and salve. There was still hope. All we needed to do was introspect. Stop, see, and listen to where we were, and why we had reached there. We needed then to tap into the energy within and begin the process of healing.

These soothing words were spoken by none other than the illustrious and renowned saint of India, Morari Bapu, who has made Ramayana his very breath and being. For Bapu, who lives in a one-room cottage in his village of Talgajarda in the district of Bhavnagar, technology came to the aid as he reached out to millions across the globe in over 170 countries.

Each day, he sat under the holy Tribhuvana Vata (banyan tree where he first began the journey of reciting Katha) on a swing and spoke for about an hour, assuring his listeners that he was with them in these trying times.

Not only did he speak about the prevailing condition but delved deeper, taking listeners on a fascinating journey into Indian mythology and spirituality.

This book is an attempt to collate all the learnings from the conversations that Morari Bapu had with his followers, whom he lovingly calls flowers, during his daily one-hour discourse. The reason one calls it conversations is because a lot of queries were mailed daily to Bapu, and many were selected and extensively answered by him, as he connected with viewers through video.

The subjects covered in the book are mostly based on Sutras (Sanskrit word for thread, but here it means meaningful extracts) rather than personal details, which were also shared by Bapu during the course of these dialogues, which he named as 'Hari Katha'.

Even though these words were spoken during an epic crisis of our times, their truth and simplicity have an enduring potency that will continue to lend value and meaning to our lives for many many years ahead. The entire discourse has, therefore, been transcribed into evocative summaries bringing out the crux of the day's theme and message.

Hope you enjoy the collection!

Index

Tap Into The Energy Within...

*T*esting times can be overcome through faith and patience.

It was a quiet morning on the 25th of March 2020. Quieter than usual. In the evening before there had come the sudden announcement of a Covid Lockdown by Prime Minister Narendra Modi in a televised address to a startled nation. Life had suddenly and abruptly come to a grinding halt now; society was yet to make an introduction with the new phenomenon of Coronavirus, and how in weeks and months ahead it would alter the connotation of everyday living. Befuddled, perplexed, and scared, serpentine queues had suddenly emerged to stock up on essentials, as humanity together stepped into an ambiguous age.

Change can be petrifying but the vagueness about the repercussions of the disease, and also on livelihood had thrown up daunting challenges externally as well as in the universe within. So, on Day 1 of this period of clouded uncertainty, renowned orator of Ramayana, Morari Bapu, offered to extend a hand of friendship and companionship. Sitting under the holy banyan tree called Tribhuvana Vata under which he had narrated his first Ram Katha, he swung slowly on his Jhoola (iron-wrought swing) as he reached out to millions through technology. Comfortably ensconced with him on his starch white cushions were two scriptures–the Ram Charita Manas and Vinay Patrika of Goswami Tulsidas.

There was no one else except the colourful swathe of his garden behind him and a few birds having a quarrel on nearby trees, blissfully unaware that the world around them had incontrovertibly transformed.

Bapu greeted listeners on the first day of the Navratra (festival) and asked everyone–from 'Swa to Sarva' (from oneself to the entire world)–to follow the necessary instructions of home confinement and social distancing for the greater good of all. And not by being scared but by being fully aware of the gravitas of the moment.

Citing the Ramayana, the spiritual leader explained how adversity tests us, and the elements that we should hold on to so as to overcome the situation. He quoted from the Ramayana:

Dheeraj Dharma Mitra Aru Nari, Aapada Kaala Parikhi Ahi Chari

(Patience, religion, friend, and a woman (here wife/companion)–these four are put to the test only in the times of adversity.)

II Ram Charita Manas–Aranya Kaand–4.4 II

These words were spoken by Sage Attri's wife Anasuiya to Sita in the Ramayana. Drawing a parallel to the prevailing situation of national crisis, Morari Bapu elucidated that the Ram Charita Manas of Goswami Tulsidas teaches us not to panic or be fearful but be patient. Elaborating on each of the four elements mentioned above, he said, "Firstly, by keeping faith on the Supreme Element, patience will emerge from within, and it will help us wade through the period," he said.

Secondly, Dharma or religion, Bapu explained, in essence could be defined as 'Truth, Love and Compassion'–the three fundamentals that will keep us steadfast during cataclysmic times.

"Thirdly, a friend–our best friend is the Supreme Element. God is attached to us through various relationships; at times God can be a friend to us like he was to Arjun...When crisis comes into our life, we should always remember that Lord Krishna is with us."

Finally, a woman is not just a feminine gender, but also refers to our inner strength or energy which is put to the test during times of adversity. Feminine energy has many meanings:

Ya Devi Sarvabhuteshu Dhruti Rupen Sansthita, Kshama Rupen Sansthita, Daya Rupen Sansthita

(Goddess Durga is an epitome of patience, forgiveness & mercy)

II Devisuktam/Chandipath-Chapter 5 Devimahatmyam II

"I even go to an extent of saying 'Ahimsa Rupen Sansthita' (feminine energy is also an embodiment of non-violence)," Bapu said.

Thus, in such turmoil, Morari Bapu requested all to keep calm and be patient, follow the path of truth, love, and compassion, safeguard our friendly bonds across the globe and tap into the energy within.

He also promised that he would meet everyone daily throughout this taxing period, bringing with him fresh insights on life, how to deal with the crisis and nuanced meanings of spirituality.

Our Endless Desires Are
The Cause Of Our Crisis

*O*ur limitless *Trishna* or *desires are the root of our own destruction. Humanity must learn how to draw boundaries to what one needs.*

"Lord Ram used 31 arrows to annihilate Ravan, but during these days of worshipping the goddess in Navratras, we hope that we will not need 31 arrows and the 21-day Lockdown period would suffice to overcome Coronavirus," said Morari Bapu. On Day 2 of Hari Katha, he urged people to treat this period as a "Tapa" (penance), which is regarded very highly in the Ram Charita Manas:

Tapabala Rachai Prapanchu Bidhata I Tapabala Bishnu Sakal Jag Trata II

Tapabala Sambhu Karahi Sanghara I Tapabala Seshu Dharai Mahibhara II

(By virtue of penance the Creator creates the universe. By virtue of penance Vishnu protects the whole world. By virtue of penance Shambhu i.e., Lord Shiva brings about dissolution. By virtue of penance, again, Shesha (the serpent god) bears the burden of the earth on his head)

II Ram Charita Manas-Bal Kaand-72.02 II

Bapu explained that penance is of three types: "Many people practice penance in Rajasi Tapa (the mode of passion), many do Tamasi Tapa (wrathful penance) and many others Satviki Tapa (serene penance). The outcome of these three categories is different."

"I feel, penance should be serene in today's era, as through it we can achieve three things. It will manifest Pramanikata (genuineness) in our heart which will lead to Pavitrata (purity) and these two will culminate into Prasannata (happiness)."

"When our soul is happy, it feels the presence of the Supreme Element."

Over expectations and multiple desires are the hurdles to happiness, he asserted.

Bapu quoted a story of a bell that could manifest anything a person desired. In the hand of a righteous man, it provided happiness because he was content with only as much as he needed. But in the hand of his brother, who was avaricious, it became the cause of his own destruction.

It is therefore important to limit our endless desires, which are the cause of the current problem. Our immoderate ways of living have clearly exacted a crisis of disproportionate proportions.

To understand this in context of the Ram Charita Manas, let us see what is written about Sita, the Supreme Goddess of the universe.

Udbhav Stithi Sanhar Karinim Klesh Harinim

Sarva Shreyaskari Sita Natoham Ramvallabham

(I bow to Sita, the beloved consort of Lord Ram, who is responsible for the creation, sustenance, and dissolution (of the universe), removes afflictions and begets all blessings)

II Ram Charita Manas–Bal Kaand–05 II

Despite being supremely great, Sita worships Mother Bhavani and seeks a boon for a 'Nija Anurupa Var'–a husband in accordance with her own capacity. Morari Bapu explained that this indicates that we must stay within our limited means rather than have limitless expectations. We must gauge our capacity and be satisfied if our general requirements are met.

In Mahabharata too when Draupadi asked Veda Vyasa whether this life is sufficient and equipped to absorb the greatest knowledge of the Supreme, Sage Vyas responded by saying that your name has been kept 'Krishna' (Draupadi was also called Krishna), but it should have been Trishna (endless desire), meaning that she finds nothing sufficient.

Whether it is the hunger for knowledge or material objects, all desires must have a boundary.

How Can We Free Ourselves From Mental Distress?

*T*he journey from distress to blessedness can be undertaken and successfully accomplished. But we must remedy some maladies for that.

The body and mind are intrinsically and intimately linked. That is a truth which Morari Bapu, espoused as he reached out to millions of people on Day 3 of Hari Katha during the Coronavirus Lockdown period.

"Because of ill health, the mind cannot remain healthy. Some self-realized souls may be exceptions to this rule; but generally speaking, physical ailments lead to mental health issues and conversely, when the mind is depressed or stressed, it has a negative impact on the body," he affirmed.

"In the Bhagavad Gita, Arjun is mentally distressed. The first chapter is about Arjun's Vishad Yoga (Arjun's distress). And the 18th chapter is called Moksha Sanyasa Yoga (a chapter pertaining to liberation). But, in my personal opinion, though the first chapter of the Gita is Vishad Yoga of Arjun (a chapter about Arjun's distress), the 18th chapter actually is Arjun's Prasad Yoga (a chapter about Arjun feeling blessed). That is because in the concluding section, Arjun says, 'Nashto Moha' (my delusion has been destroyed) and through Krishna's compassion and grace, he is feeling healthy again."

Bapu explained that it is a well-known fact that Arjun was an exceptional personality, whom Lord Krishna has called his *Vibhuti* (ornament) among Pandavas as also his Ishta (deity/subject of worship) and Priya (dearly loved). Arjun had extraordinary abilities and many feats of stupendous courage to his credit.

Yet, seeing his loved ones on the battlefield of Kurukshetra, he is deeply distressed. Because of the mental agony of having to take on friends and relatives in war, his body parts are impacted. Arjun says that his body is shivering, flesh is burning, and the Gandiva (name of Arjun's bow) is slipping from his hand. Morari Bapu, thus, wondered that if this was the condition of a man so accomplished, what can be said of ordinary persons like us?

Linking it to the prevailing crisis of the Coronavirus epidemic, Bapu said that we are living in a highly disturbed environment; it is only natural that people will feel physically ill. "When the epidemic has gripped everyone, the world needs Prasad or Grace," he added.

In Ram Charita Manas' last canto Uttar Kaand, Garuda asks seven questions to the crow saint Bhusundi, of which the final one pertains to mental health. Garuda too wants to know that when even eminent personalities can be afflicted, what could be a possible solution to stay healthy and positive.

It is in this very interesting conversation that the remedy to rid oneself of mental ailments is embedded. Bhusundi, the crow saint, says that a man is freed from all mental illnesses through Ram Kripa i.e., the Grace of God. And the doctor to administer such a remedy is a Sadaguru or a Buddhpurush (realized soul). Such a saint is beyond the boundaries created by caste, creed, and country.

Rama kripa nasahi saba roga, jau ehi bhati banai sanyoga

Sadagura baida bacana bisvasa, sanjama yaha na bisaya kai asa

Raghupati bhagati sajivana muri, anupana sraddha mati puri

(All these ailments can no doubt be eradicated if by Sri Ram's grace the following factors combine. There must be faith in the words of the physician in the form of a true preceptor, and the regimen is indifference to the pleasures of sense. Devotion to the Lord of the Raghus is the life-giving herb; while a devout mind serves as the vessel in which it is partaken.)

II Ram Charita Manas–Uttar Kaand–122 II

It is apparent from these words of Goswami Tulsidas that the condition for the remedy to be effective is that we must have faith in the words of a Self-Realized soul.

Morari Bapu then urged that we need to introspect whether the Covid-19 epidemic had been triggered by our excesses and 'Visehey Sevan' (over-indulgence in materialistic pleasures).

"We have disturbed Nature–the rivers, sky, air, forests. Our body is made of five elements, and we have tortured them all. Now is the time to show restraint and become more temperate in our ways of living."

Moderate and balanced life in turn will make us a subject of God's grace.

Further, we need to ponder over the query that when we cannot gauge the mind another person, how can we know what is in the womb of the future. Vedas have also said–Neti, Neti, Neti (not this, not this, not this–means there is more to it than this).

In such a scenario, moderation in our ways and devotion towards the Supreme can deliver us.

And in terms of the proof on whether the medicine is working, and we are on the way to recovery, Bapu said that just like a person suffering from sickness starts feeling hungry when his health improves, similarly our 'Sumati Chhudha'(hunger for good thinking) increases–meaning our interest in sensory pleasures starts waning and we don't feel trapped in a web of endless desires. After this detachment starts setting in.

Jania taba mana biruja gosai, jaba ura bala biraga adhikai

Sumati chudha barhai nita nai, bisaya asa durbalata gai

Bimala gyana jala jaba so nahai, taba raha rama bhagati ura chai

(The mind should be accounted as cured, my lord, only when the heart gathers strength in the form of dispassion, appetite in the shape of good resolutions grows stronger and stronger every day, and weakness in the form of sensual appetite diminishes. Being thus rid of all diseases, when the soul bathes in the pure water of wisdom, the heart is saturated with devotion to Sri Ram.)

II Ram Charita Manas-Uttar Kaand-122 II

This then is the entire journey from being mentally distressed to feeling blessed and experiencing peace.

How Can You Identify A True Guru?

A *great saint can be a great facilitator in our spiritual journey. But what are the traits of such a Master?*

Stillness of the night, the silver moon and sparkling stars can touch a soul much like the cool breeze swings a bloom. As per the Yoga Vashishtha Maha Ramayana, every element of the universe is a life-giving herb–the sun, the spray of the great Ganges and the leaf of the revered Tulsi. They act as medicine for humans who are afflicted with the maladies of over-indulgence. The biggest panacea though remains the chanting of God's name.

On Day 4 of Hari Katha, Morari Bapu quoted this great text comprising 32,000 Sanskrit couplets that describe these remedies for the worst of physical and psychological ailments that we suffer. Brahma or God is also the cure as is the being in the attendance of saints and a Guru.

But how does one identify a true saint or a spiritual master in whose company our malaises will be dissipated? Bapu said that a Guru is not merely represented by saffron robes or through a cult or by personality worship, a guru is epitomised by his thoughts, words, and conduct. His manner of living should be so pure that it becomes a subject of veneration itself.

Morari Bapu then quoted Lord Ram who tells Shabari in the Ram Charita Manas:

Prathama bhagatis santana kar sanga, doosri rati mum katha prasanga

(The first in order of devotion is fellowship with the saints and the second is marked by a fondness for my stories.)

II Ram Charita Manas–Aranya Kaand-35 II

As per Bapu, a Guru as mentioned in such a context must be symbolic of:

1. The colour blue-he must have large heartedness and the vastness of the sky. He cannot be narrow-minded.

2. The colour red-symbolises bravery, love, and patience. And true love cannot exist without courage.

3. Green-for internal and external prosperity and his Shiv Sankalpa (determined effort) for the welfare of others.

4. Yellow-for purity of thoughts, words, and action.

5. Black-for Udasinta (detachment and dispassion). Such a person is not Udas (unhappy) while living amidst society but in solitude he always remains unattached.

6. White-for peace. A guru must be peaceful and have the ability to bring peace to others.

A sage with such attributes can fit the description of a true Guru. A great master is always absorbed in the Self and remains in constant remembrance of the Supreme. He is satisfied in every circumstance and participates in holy congregations.

Morari Bapu then narrated a tale often quoted by the Bauls (roaming mendicants of Bengal). There were two birds in a cage. They conspire to escape and with continuous effort create enough impact to squeeze out of the grill. One bird immediately flies out while the second stays back, as it is determined to destroy its coop.

The spiritual meaning of the anecdote is that a true saint will never condemn this world as a prison but teach us how to achieve liberation. He does not teach us to destroy; rather he gives us wings.

Such a person, as described above in a multitude of ways and colours, can truly be called a Guru or a Spiritual Master.

Secret Key Of Everlasting Happiness

*A*di Shankaracharya said that solitude is the key to happiness. In circumstances of enforced isolation like that during Coronavirus lockdown, can our cup of joy still overflow?

Once speaking at the inauguration of a chair at Surat University dedicated to Osho, spiritual guru Morari Bapu expanded to give a different dynamic to the meaning of the acronym 'OSHO'. He felt OSHO should mean–"Own Silent, Happiness Own", meaning our silence and peace should be internal and within us.

The great Adi Shankaracharya had said, '*Ekante Sukhamasyatam*' (*there is happiness in solitude*). On Day 5 of Hari Katha, Bapu felt that considering the Lockdown has naturally put us in a situation of solitude, we must use it for the purpose of introspection.

"Is the peace that we feel really our own? Silence can be of many kinds. There is a deep hush even in a graveyard. Sometimes we become quiet due to the compulsions of our circumstances. Sometimes a wicked man can force us into silence by showing us fear," Bapu said.

He explained further, "A child plays with toys and then discards them. He understands that toys are meant for him, and he is not meant for the toy."

The same is true of material objects in life. "We need to analyse whether our happiness is based on some incident, object, person, country, or time. A Buddhpurush (realized soul) is in bliss all the time because he is the reason for his own happiness. The joy is neither borrowed nor purchased or dependent on external factors. This is inner peace."

We could use time when we are confined to our homes and with limited social mingling to internally analyse these aspects and we might find new strength.

"What is not yours and is borrowed is never permanent. It will break or be interrupted..."

The Ramayana says:

Nija sukha binu mana hoi ki thira, parasa ki hoi bihina sameera

(Can the mind be stilled without inner happiness? Just like there can be no touch without the existence of air.)

II Ram Charita Manas–Uttar Kaand–90 (A) II

This brings us to the question of whether we all can find that calm within.

Morari Bapu feels that in actuality there is no difference between a Guru and the disciple except it being a societal arrangement. Only that the disciple's internal lamp needs to be lit. Fundamentally, they are the same in the spiritual realm, otherwise Adi Shankaracharya would not have said, *"Na Bandhur Na Mitram Guru Naiva Shishyah, Chidaananda Rupah Shivoham Shivoham."* (I am not the relative, nor the friend, nor the guru, nor the disciple. I am indeed, that eternal knowing and bliss, Shiva, love, and pure consciousness.)

"Goswami Tulsidas also says 'Shrota Vakta Gyan Nidhi (both the listener and narrator of God's tale are full of knowledge)– in truth both are on the same plane."

"Guru only enters into a disciple's life and lights the lamp of his soul and in the light of this lamp, all delusion is destroyed!"

And what do we discover after such a stage?

"God is all about acceptance and love. God is the joy within and the peace that emanates from within us. They are synonyms," Bapu said emphatically.

Five Modern-Day Yagnas That Can Uplift You

The five yagnas as described in the Bhagavad Gita can be interpreted in the current context and used to sharpen and enhance our human qualities.

The Bhagavad Gita has recommended five yagnas for human beings. These five include Dravya (donation of wealth), Tapa (penance), Yoga, Swadhyaya (self-learning), and Gyana (acquisition of knowledge).

On Day 6 of Hari Katha, Morari Bapu cited these five but gave them a meaning contextual to our times, especially in the period when Coronavirus gripped the world. He started by saying that yagna itself means 'Swaha' (to give up) and not just 'Wah Wah' (our desire for recognition).

Bapu said that during the Lockdown period, people should conduct five yagnas that will remain pertinent in a unique way even in the future.

Dravya (donation of wealth): Donate towards the cause of alleviation of Covid-19. Bapu also appreciated that a lot of people had come forward to help the poor and needy. Otherwise as well, Bapu emphasises on donating 10% of one's total earnings towards worthy causes.

Tapa (penance): We should keep an even temperament though we may be frustrated by being confined to our homes or for any other reason. We must treat this as penance and take inspiration from Shiva, who in Ram Charita Manas is shown as sitting under one tree for a long period indicating his highly stable state. When we remove too many 'Tark-Vitaraka' (debates and arguments), we too get established in faith.

Yoga (yoga's literal meaning is conjoining): Staying isolated and away from friends and families during Covid caused 'Viyoga' (separation). We also experienced, in one sense, 'Sanyoga' i.e., were bound to one place. We should therefore have done 'Upyoga' i.e., put our abilities to the best use.

Swadhyaya (self-learning): We can spend our time usefully by going through our sacred texts and learning from them. We can also do 'Swa Ka Adhyanan' i.e., self-introspection. We must evaluate our personalities and recognize our strengths and weaknesses and work on areas of improvement.

Gyana (acquisition of knowledge): 'Information' is a route while 'knowledge' is the destination. In times of 'Yantrana' (pain), it is important to do 'Vicharna' (give adequate thought) that helps us to develop the understanding that we must move from the limits of 'Swa' (oneself) and work for 'Sarva' i.e., welfare of all. We must reach this state of understanding or 'Gyana'.

The Ram Katha exponent further explained that we need to realize that a Covid-like situation has arisen in the first place due to an imbalance. Inanimate or gross objects are for our utilization while the animate world is for loving. What humans have done is exactly the opposite as they have fallen in love with inanimate objects like wealth and exploited animals and other humans for selfish means.

Bapu said that excessive 'Asha'(desires) have become our 'Pasha'(chains) that have entangled us. We have moved away from Nature and God.

It is said that chanting of the holy name can free us from all internal and external ailments, Bapu concluded. Let us lean on the name of God to free ourselves from fear of the future, and the pain of the past.

By doing these five yagnas, we can make the journey from 'Swa Iccha' to 'Sarva Ke Liye Iccha' i.e., move away from narrow self-interest and think about the well-being of the world at large.

Why Do We Face Dualities Like Joy-Pain And Gain-Loss?

*T*here are four main reasons why we face a cycle of events in our lives. Of these, three factors are mostly inevitable, but there is one which we have the power to mould.

Life is a web of unending dualities–happiness–grief, gain–loss, auspicious–inauspicious, good health–ailments, and the like. The question then arises, what is the root cause of all these dichotomies?

Many people feel that all that we endure in the world is because of our Karma. While this is true, there is a more elaborate perspective that is offered on Day 7 of Hari Katha by Morari Bapu based on the Ramayana, a text that he is famous for singing and explaining.

As per Bapu, there are four major factors behind these dualities. And we are all, in one sense, trussed by these.

1. Kaal (time): Just like we feel cold in winters and hot in summers, and rains bring humidity, in the same way what we experience is in a large part dependent on the time phase we exist in. The cycle of Kalyuga is considered the epoch that we are occupying currently. Kalyuga too has an impact on our actions which, in this particular time period, are driven by self-interest to such a great extent

that we have become exploitative and entangled in unethical deeds. Even the Bhagavad Gita says that there is only one eternal truth and that is Kaal, which here means death.

2. Karma (actions): As per Hindu thought, there are constant cameras on each person and there are invisible witnesses like the Dishas (directions), sun, moon etc. to all our actions. Our soul is a mute spectator to what we do. By constantly participating in holy congregations, we develop the power of 'Vivek' i.e., discretion about what is right and wrong, and which actions will prove to be good or counter-productive for us.

Karma pradhana bisva kari rakha, jo jasa karahai so tas phalu chakha

(He has made Karma the ruling factor in this world, so that one reaps what one sows)

II Ram Charita Manas-Ayodhya Kaand-219 II

3. Gunas (characteristics): The best state is said to be that of being Gunatita (beyond the state of Gunas), however, it is very difficult to reach such a stage. We must therefore understand that actions done in Satva Guna (the mode of goodness) bring us peace and happiness while those done in Rajoguna (the mode of passion) and Tamo Guna (the mode of ignorance) take us towards destruction. Guna in Sanskrit means rope, which indicates that Gunas are ultimately a cause of bondage, and we must try to liberate ourselves from them.

4. Swabhava (temperament): Our own nature can be the biggest cause of our pain and also for those who are

associated with us and interact with us. It is common human behaviour to constantly evaluate others and pass comments and judgements on them. However, we fail to self-introspect and find out our own failings. Am I short-tempered? Am I prone to negativity, do I criticise others? Am I harsh and rude? Do I get jealous and envious? Such questions and more need to be pondered over, Bapu urged.

About Lord Ram's temperament, it is said by Goswami Tulsidas:

Jasu subhau arihi anukula, so kimi karihi matu pratikula

(How could he whose temperament was congenial even to an enemy act contrary to the will of his own mother?)

II Ram Charita Manas-Ayodhya Kaand-32 II

The reason why Ramayana continues to stir us is that it is an elaborate commentary of Lord Ram's disposition which is pleasing to all and inspires us.

Ram Katha proponent Morari Bapu then explained that, as per his thinking, if we can maintain a balance in the first three (Kaal, Karma and Gunas mentioned above), their impact can be blunted. It must also be understood that these three are beyond our control, so their consequences need to be endured. The key is thus to remain equipoised.

However, it is the fourth one Swabhava, that is in our own hands. We must constantly think about our temperament and its shortcomings. And work upon our failings and improve our behaviour to bring peace to ourselves as also to those around us and become more and more attuned with Mother Nature and the Divine.

When Faced With A Problem, Resort To These Three Solutions

Wʰen in crisis, here is what you can do...

In the Ramayana, the character of Ravan is one of the most prominent and central to the narrative. On Day 8 of Hari Katha, Morari Bapu said Ravan can be likened to delusion and darkness. By one interpretation he can also be described as a 'Maharoga' (pandemic), so much so that an analogy can be drawn with the Coronavirus that wreaked havoc across the globe.

If one were to study the text of Ram Charita Manas by Goswami Tulsidas, Ravan after severe penance gets a boon that ensures him near immortality. He becomes so powerful and arrogant that he torments the world and there is much uproar owing to his atrocities.

Atisaya dekhi dharma kai glani, parama sabhita dhara akulani

giri sari sindhu bhar nahi mohi, jasa mohi garua eka paradrohi

sakala dharma dekhai biparita, kahi na sakai Ravana bhaya bhita

dhenu rupa dhari hridaya bicari, gai taha jaha sura muni jhari

nija santapa sunaesi roi, kahu te kachu kaja na hoi

(Perceiving the supreme disrespect for religion, Earth was extremely alarmed and perturbed. The weight of mountains, rivers, and oceans, she said, is not so oppressive to me as of him who is malevolent to others. She saw all goodness perverted; yet for fear of Ravan, she could not utter a word. After great deliberation she took the form of a cow and went to the site where all gods and sages were in hiding. With tears in her eyes, she told them her sufferings; but none of them could be of any aid to her."

II Ram Charita Manas–Bal Kaand–184 II

As per the scripture, the gods, sages and Gandharvas (celestial songsters), all then repaired to Brahma's abode; with them was poor Earth in the form of a cow grievously stricken with fear and grief. Brahma came to know everything; and realizing in his heart of heart his inability to help her, he said, "The immortal Lord whose servant you are will be my help as well as yours."

Dharani dharahi mana dhira kaha biranci haripada sumiru,

janata jana ki pira prabhu bhanjihi daruna bipati.

("Have patience, Earth," said Brahma, "and fix your mind on the feet of Sri Hari. The Lord knows the distress of His servants and will put an end to your terrible suffering.")

II Ram Charita Manas–Bal Kaand–Soratha 184 II

The story goes that all the gods then sat in counsel and wondered where to find God. While different suggestions were being forwarded, Lord Shiva advised that God is omnipresent and ever-present and can be revealed by love even as fire is manifested by friction.

Sure enough, as the deities entreated God in unison, a deep voice came from heaven, which removed all their doubt and anxiety and assured them that He would take avatar and end their miseries. And as the gods waited patiently for Him to reveal himself on earth, they all were called upon Brahma to appear in the form of monkeys and bears to aid in God's endeavour to eliminate Ravan.

This episode holds important lessons for anyone faced with a distressing crisis. We too can resort to these three solutions in a sequence as has been elaborated above:

1. Pursharath (proactively work for a solution): Let us not become indolent and work towards the cause of the removal of the problem.

2. Pukaar (prayer): Call out for help.

3. Pratiskha (wait patiently): Have patience that will help us wade over the predicament.

Procedure Of How God Can Appear In Our Life

*T*he birth of Ram as encapsulated in the Ram Charita Manas has several spiritual connotations that can be applied to our lives.

Lord Ram is without a parallel. He is the ultimate truth, as per our scriptures. He is like the vast sky that holds innumerable stars, the moon, and the sun; yet it remains untouched. But if one thinks deeply, even this sky emanates from the Supreme Power. This is what Morari Bapu espoused on Day 9 of Hari Katha.

He elaborated on the learnings obtained from ancient seers– from the sky appeared the air and from the air, fire was born. Fire was the source of water and water in turn of the earth, which led to the harvest of food grains, which nurtures the human body. And within the temple of our body resides Ram or what one can describe as the Supreme Element of the universe.

Morari Bapu explained that it is from Lord Ram that everything manifests and into whom everything submerges. In the Bal Kaand, which is the first canto of the Ram Charita Manas, Lord Ram's mother Kausalya says:

"Brahmnda nikaya nirmita maya rom rom prati beda kahai,"

(The Vedas proclaim that every pore of Your body contains multitudes of universes brought forth by Maya (illusion).)

II Ram Charita Manas-Baal Kaand-Chhand 192 II

About His avatar on Earth as captured in the Ramayana, the story goes that there was a mighty emperor of Ayodhya called Dasratha, who remained childless till an advanced age in life.

As years passed, anxiety about the future of his kingdom gripped the king and he approached his Guru, Vishistha, about the pain of being childless.

"Eka bar bhupati mana mahi, bhai galani more suta nahi.

Gura griha gayau turata mahipala, charana lagi kari binaya bisala.1."

(One day the king was sad at heart that he had no son. He hastened to his preceptor's residence and, falling at his feet, made many entreaties.)

II Ram Charita Manas-Baal Kaand-Ch 188 II

Sage Vishistha assured him of a resolution and organised a yagna from whose flames emerged a bowl of a sweet dish which was partaken by the three main consorts of the king and caused them to successfully bear children.

There are many spiritual meanings to this incident. First and foremost, the birth of Ram takes place in Ayodhya.

What does 'Awadh' (Ayodhya) connote? It means-"Jaha wadh na ho"-where there is no assault on anyone through mind, words, and body. A place that is free from conflict and brimming with humaneness; it is in such a space that God manifests.

In such a kingdom reigns Dasratha. The spiritual allusion of Dasratha is the 'Jeev Atma' that is the soul, who is holding the reins of 'Das Ratha'-ten chariots of our sense organs and whose 'Su Gati' (good stead and actions) leads us to 'Su Laksh' (ultimate goal).

But there is an eleventh element which is 'Mun' (mind) which made Dasratha feel distressed of the vacuum of not having any progeny.

Spiritually analysing, 'Haani' (loss/damage) is external while 'Galani' (deep pain or guilt) is internal. Bapu's grandfather Tribhuvana Das ji had taught him, "Go to Govind when you either feel Haani or Galani; particularly Galani, as it is a deeply personal feeling, it should not be shared with just about anyone."

The fact that a yagna was organised is indicative of the meaning that we must first do 'Swaha' of 'Wah-Wah' or give up everything else to obtain bliss.

That Dasratha's Guru organised a ceremony that led to the birth of Ram shows that we cannot find God through our means or efforts, but only through a Realized Master's grace.

Just before the ceremony, there is an episode in which Lord Shiva tells other deities that God can be obtained only through love and devotion.

"Hari vyapaka sarvatra samana, prem te paragat hoe main jana"

(The Lord always manifests Himself in response to the devotion and love one cherishes in one's heart.)

II Ram Charita Manas–Baal Kaand–Ch 185 II

When Ram appears before his mother Kausalya, she looks bewilderingly at his transcendental form and requests him to appear in the human figure. Further, she asks him to become a child and then further like a baby, who cries at birth. As per Morari Bapu this entire sequence is a process just like Ram Charita Manas is a complete procedure to make us more humane.

When we inculcate the qualities that were in Dasratha and emulate his actions as described above, then divinity can appear in our lives too.

It is also said that God appears for the protection of Dharma, cows, and deities. This means he comes to give the four fruits of human life. He not only establishes righteousness–Dharma, but also provides 'Artha' (wealth) which was comparable with cows in earlier periods, 'Kama' (fulfilment of desires) which is a prominent feature among 'Devatas' (deities) and Moksha i.e., Nirvana.

Ram Charita Manas, written by Goswami Tulsidas, is a beautiful scripture encapsulating the life of Lord Ram. The happy coincidence is that Ram Charita Manas was also completed on Ram Navami and thus the day is considered not just as the birth date of Ram but also of the Ramayana.

"Naumi bhauma bara madhu masa, avadhapuri yaha charita prakasa

Jehi dina Ram janam Shruti gavahi, tiratha sakala taha chali avahi.3."

(On Tuesday, the ninth of the lunar month of Chaitra, this story spread its lustre at Ayodhya. On this day of Sri Ram's birth, the presiding spirits of all holy places flock there.)

II Ram Charita Manas-Baal Kaand-Ch 34 II

Eight Desires Of Human Life...And How To Fulfil Them

*H*uman *beings have a constant wish list in life. But most desires fall into eight basic categories. Here is how we must interpret them and take them to fruition.*

Desire is an intrinsic part of human life. We all wish for a variety of things; many are materialistic and some emotional. We want health, wealth, comfort, good relationships, success, good progeny, and fame. There are also spiritual desires–we want to know about life after death, about how to remain detached and equanimous under all circumstances and we want to be at peace. But these myriad wishes arise from some basic human desires. On Day 10 of Hari Katha, Morari Bapu, analysed these eight innate contraptions of human want:

1. Shanti: Peace

2. Shakti: Strength

3. Gyana: Knowledge

4. Swatantra: Freedom

5. Saundarya: Beauty

6. Amaratva: Immortality

7. Anand: Bliss

8. Prem: Love

Morari Bapu explained how Ram Charita Manas through different sequences shows how these desires can be fulfilled as per our 'Patrata' (eligibility). He explained these sequentially.

PEACE, STRENGTH AND KNOWLEDGE

Shantam sasvatamaprameyamanagha nirvanashantipradam

(Ram-the bestower of supreme peace in the form of final beatitude, placid, eternal, beyond the ordinary means of cognition, sinless and all-pervading.)

II Ram Charita Manas-Sundar Kaand-Shloka 1 II

In the first Shloka of Sundar Kaand, Lord Ram has been described as the bestower of peace and it is to Him and his holy name that we need to turn to obtain serenity of mind.

Another basic characteristic we would need to imbibe in our endeavour is to take refuge at the feet of a spiritual master. Our strength will emerge from our complete surrender to a Guru. And such a strength that emanates from a spiritual master is superior to personal power as it is free from ego.

Not only physical strength, Ram Charita Manas explains that intellectual prowess or knowledge is also a form of power.

Dana parasu budhi shakti pracanda, bara bigyana kathina kodanda.4.

(Again, charity is the axe; reason, the fierce lance and the highest wisdom, the relentless bow.)

II Ram Charita Manas-Lanka Kaand-Ch 80 (A) II

In addition to a sharp mind, if we have 'Nirmal Mati' (uncontaminated thinking), it can lead us to 'Vishram' or peace.

Takey juga pad kamal manavu, jasu kripa nirmal mati pavau 4.

(I seek to propitiate the pair of Her (Sita's) lotus feet, so that by Her grace I may be blessed with a refined intellect.)

II Ram Charita Manas–Bal Kaand–Ch 18 II

FREEDOM

To remain dependent upon or under the protection of a Guru can provide us with real freedom.

Ram gives Bharat full freedom to choose the way forward after the demise of their father Dasratha, but Bharat chooses to choose whatever Ram chooses.

Bharat shows complete surrender as he pleads:

Jehi bidhi prabhu prasan mun hoi, karuna sagar kijiye soi 1.

(Do that, O ocean of mercy, which may please your heart, my lord.)

II Ram Charita Manas–Ayodhya Kaand–Ch 269 II

BEAUTY AND IMMORTALITY

Beauty should not be seen as only externally extant but must emerge as an inner magnificence. And immortality should be interpreted not just by the measure that we are alive. The quality of our thoughts and our contribution to add to the vitality of the world during a lifetime also insinuate immortality.

LOVE AND BLISS

Immortality can be understood only by those who are ready to consume poison (hardship, criticism, etc.) like Mira.

Sacrifice is a by-product of love, which in turn helps us obtain bliss.

However, anyone who is free from these desires can be called a Sanyasi (ascetic). In the Bhagavad Gita, Lord Krishna in his address to Arjun defines such a person as Nitya Sanyasi who holds no malice for anyone, neither does he desire anything.

Fundamentals Of Prayer

There are some daily prayers that are recommended by the Hindu scriptures, but these also hold a sublime meaning. Moreover, we must give an additional dimension to our daily supplications during trying times.

Prayer is a deeply personal affair. It is the communication between us and the Supreme Power, wherein we express our fears, desires, and gratitude. During the 11th Day of Hari Katha, Morari Bapu, delved into the Sanatana Dharma's tradition of praying to the five supreme elements. Adi Shankaracharya instructed Hindus to pray to Lord Surya, Lord Ganesha, Lord Shiva, Lord Vishnu, and Goddess Parvati. The prayer to these five major powers holds a profound and sublime meaning.

- Bapu explained that while it is good to do Surya Puja or pray to Sun God daily, we must endeavour to lead a life full of light and awakening.

- By praying to Ganesha, it means that we must inculcate Vivek or the power of discretion about how to act in our lives.

- We must work towards the welfare of all, which is the prime trait of Lord Shiva.

- Lord Vishnu indicates a certain largesse; our vision too should be broad, and we must cultivate the quality of large-heartedness.

- And like Goddess Parvati, we must be full of devotion to God.

Continuing the discourse, Morari Bapu then went on to the subject of adoration of one's Guru. On being asked why there was so much importance given to Guru Ruj (dust of a Guru's feet or sandals), Bapu explained that these particles of dust are sufficient for a disciple, as a very small amount of a true Master's grace can ripen a follower spiritually.

It is not within our power to want more, as the amount of energy in a Realized Master is so much that our body cannot absorb it. We can never reach that stage of eligibility where we can fully understand the extent of a Guru's greatness.

Regarding prayer that we can offer to our Divine Master, his 'Smruti' or remembrance at all times is of prime importance.

The greatest service we can extend to him is by full obeying his instructions and imbibing his teachings.

We must continue to see God in all living beings around us and also in inanimate objects as the entire universe is throbbing with divinity.

Bapu then recommended that during the phase of Coronavirus, we must add 5 pujas/prayers. These should be:

1. Deh Puja-We must take all precautions to look after our bodies

2. Deen Puja-We must help those who are without resources

3. Desh Seva-We must do whatever we can do in the service of the nation

4. Dev Seva-We must remember the holiest element of our life

5. Dil Seva-We must serve ourselves and our soul

Sage Patanjali's Four Simple Sutras For Everlasting Peace

Everyone wants to be happy, but most people are always stressed or depressed. Sage Patanjali resolves the quandary.

Adi Shankaracharya famously said, *"Prasanna chitte paramatma darshanam"*–the door to God is a happy state of mind. However, in the modern world we all face extreme stress, depression, and distress. As much as we want to be in a joyous frame of mind, we find ourselves in the opposite state of mental health.

Explaining the simple four-pronged formula of Bhagvana Patanjali to stay happy, Morari Bapu on Day 12 of Hari Katha explained that as Albert Einstein is the scientist of the external world, Patanjali is a scientist of our internal world.

Bapu elaborated, "Unhappiness is a very big disease. And there are few scriptures like that of Sage Patanjali which are as appropriate as a solution to achieve a blissful state of mind, and so sufficient if we follow them."

Sage Patanjali's advice in the Yoga Sutra will not only help us outgrow a state of despondency but is 'Ayush Vardhak Aushadi' i.e., acts like a life-giving medicinal herb that energises us and brings calm to our lives.

1. Sukh-Maitri: Whenever you see happiness, do friendship. This means we should derive joy from another person's happiness irrespective of whether we consider him our own or an outsider. The difficulty is that we feel envious or jealous of other people's prosperity and progress. A bigger problem still is that we are not glad even in the happiness of our own family and friends, leave alone those who are indifferent or inimical to us. This is a common trait. Slowly, inculcating the habit to wish others well will in turn bring a sense of well-being to the self.

2. Dukh-Karuna: Be compassionate whenever you see despair in the world. Again, it does not matter who is the person affected–a friend, a foe or stranger. We need to be cautious of our ego here as it sometimes prevents us from feeling empathy for others.

3. Punya-Mudita: Wherever you see a person involved in good work, find pleasure in it. Whether it is moral action or a positive verbal expression, we should appreciate and encourage it. Our competitiveness and ego prevent us from valuing and welcoming beneficial work which is being done by others. We must realize, we are all united as a part of the same creation and therefore must rejoice in the virtuous behaviour of others and their actions for the good of society.

4. Paap-Upeksha: Whenever you see or hear an act of sin, reject it. We should not reject the sinner but his act. There is always a root cause for every action. We must destroy the source of the sin and not insult the sinner.

These simple four sutras will keep us perennially happy and in a state of peace.

Identifying Three Supreme Elements In Lord Hanuman

*L*ord Hanuman is one of the most worshipped deities of Hinduism. What makes him so great and venerated?

On Day 13 of Hari Katha, Morari Bapu talked about one of Hinduism's most loved deities, Hanuman. He is the prime aide of Lord Ram and carries out a multitude of onerous tasks in the Ramayana for him.

Morari Bapu profoundly reveres Hanuman and speaks eloquently of his unmatched qualities. Bapu, who each year celebrates Hanuman Jayanti at Chitrakoot Dham, Talgajarda in Bhavnagar district of Gujarat, flawlessly articulated the qualities that make Hanuman a personality worth emulating.

"I would like to share the form in which I have experienced 'Hanumant Tatva' (Hanuman's elemental qualities). Hanuman ji is a confluence of three-three major facets."

Elaborating further, Bapu said that the power of three is great in both material and metaphysical terms. "Like Tri Satya, Tridev, Triloka, Tribhuvana, Tri Kaala and Triveni."

In Lord Hanuman too, three compounds perfectly converge:

1. Ram Naam-Constant chanting of the name of God

2. Ram Kaam-The execution of the Lord's work

3. Ram Dhaam–The Supreme's residence

Explaining, Morari Bapu said that we must cultivate the habit of chanting the name of God like Hanuman. And just as Maruti accomplished great feats for Lord Ram, we too must endeavour to not be lazy and work towards the welfare of all.

Bapu felt that if we inculcate the attribute of constant chanting of the Holy Name, we inevitably will start working for the larger good. The importance of both these attributes cannot be understated. If seen in the context of the Ram Charita Manas, Hanuman censures Vibhishana in Lanka, saying that though you repeat the name of God incessantly, you are not doing any of his work (in terms of helping to free Sita from the clutches of Ravan).

On the part about Ram Dhaam, Bapu said that not only did Hanuman live with Lord Ram in Ayodhya, but he also perfected himself to a stage wherein he himself became the residence of Lord Ram.

Pranavau pavana kumar khala bana pavaka gyana ghana, jasu hridaya agara basahiu Rama sara capa dhara

(I greet Hanuman, the son of the wind god, an embodiment of wisdom, who is fire as it were for the forest of the wicked, and in the abode of whose heart resides Sri Ram, equipped with a bow and arrows.)

II Ram Charita Manas–Bal Kaand–Soratha 17 II

The above line indicates that so great is Hanuman's Dham 'Nishta' (faith) that he himself becomes the Dham (pilgrimage).

In a subtle sense, Bapu explained that Ram can also be a synonym for the place of his dwelling, meaning Ram is where his residence is. "*Awadh Taha Jaha Ram Nivasu*–wherever Ram lives, there is Ayodhya". We can look at this concept, therefore, in a perceptive sense as well.

Hanuman is also the amalgamation of Satyam (truth) of Ram, Shivam (welfare of all) of Shankar and Sundaram (beauty) of Sita.

As Hanuman is the son of Pawan (Vayu Dev), he has Sugandh (fragrance). Because he is the avatar of Shankar, he is a Sadaguru. And his nature is Sheetal (calming), as admitted by Sita when she first meets him sitting in Lanka under the Ashok tree. So, he has these three qualities as well.

"Obtaining Hanuman means obtaining Ram himself," Bapu claimed emphatically.

When Ram withdraws into River Sarayu along with the citizens of Ayodhya, Hanuman was the lone person left on Earth with a boon to exist till Ram Katha is recited on the planet.

As an interesting insight to conclude, Bapu said that on the battlefield of Kurukshetra when Lord Krishna narrates Bhagavad Gita to Arjun, the primary listener of the Gita was actually Hanuman, who was sitting on top of the flag mast of the chariot.

Lord Hanuman was born on the Anjaneri mountain to a heavenly damsel Anjana, who was married to Kesari, the son of Brihaspati. It is believed that Anjana had performed intense prayers for 12 years to obtain offspring and was finally blessed with Shiva's incarnation as her child.

How Lord Hanuman Can Help Us On Our Spiritual Journey

*L*ord Hanuman can hold a unique and valuable position in our spiritual pursuit.

In the spiritual universe, there exists a triangle of great significance. It comprises: 1. Sant (saint) 2. Hanumant (Lord Hanuman) and 3. Bhagvant (God). For us to be able to make steady progress on the path, Morari Bapu, on Day 14 of Hari Katha, said one should keep Lord Hanuman right at the centre.

Hanuman Chalisa says, "*Tumhare bhajan Ram ko pave*"–this loosely translates to mean that by invoking Lord Hanuman, one can achieve the Supreme Power. It is also said of Hanuman that he is the guard at God's door–'*Ram dware tum rakhvare*'.

Hanuman acts like a Sadaguru in the life of a disciple. Morari Bapu explained that in the Ram Charita Manas, there are four living beings who went against Lord Shiva. The first was his wife Sati, the second was Kama Dev, the third was his father-in-law Dakhsa, and the last was Bhusundi in the Mahakal Temple. While the first three suffer, Bhusundi is saved due to the grace of his guru.

We are constantly making mistakes, but if we have a Sadaguru like Hanuman in our lives, we can be salvaged. That is why Bapu places Hanuman at the top within the spiritual triumvirate.

As for his personal attributes, Hanuman is a Brahmachari; this doesn't just mean that he is celibate but also that he is constantly absorbed in the thought of Brahma and sees God in everything around him–whether it is the trees, birds, or rivers. Whatever worldly work he may be engaged in, he has an uninterrupted flow of thought about God.

Hanuman is also Vanchari (dweller of the forest) due to his monkey body, but Vanchari also means he is Udaseen (unattached), as per Bapu. He is someone who is involved in penance and dispassion.

And in Vinay Patrika, Goswami Tulsidas has described him as Dharmachari (follower of the righteous path). Dharma here should be taken to mean 'Truth, Love and Compassion', as per Bapu's interpretation.

Explaining the concept of Dharma further, Morari Bapu said that there are some negatives attached to the primary fruits of life:

- The taint of Dharma is the expectation of returns for being righteous.

- The taint of Artha is the unnecessary accumulation of wealth.

- The taint of Kama is an extreme desire that takes us towards immoderation in seeking sensual pleasures.

Whoever is free from these extremes and taints mentioned above, obtains pure salvation–Nirvana.

Lord Hanuman is free from all these three and is thus forever liberated.

Three Characteristics To Build A Wholesome Personality

*H*ere are the attributes that we must develop to live our lives fully. All these are found aplenty in the monkey god Hanuman.

There is an interesting sequence that Morari Bapu narrated on Day 15 of Hari Katha. He said that it is believed that Hanuman Chalisa is the synopsis of Sundar Kaand and the canto is in turn the synopsis of the Ram Charita Manas.

In the Hanuman Chalisa, Goswami Tulsidas asks Lord Hanuman to bless us with three attributes–'*Bal, Buddhi, Vidya Dehi Mohe*':

1. Bal: Strength
2. Buddhi: Intelligence
3. Vidya: Knowledge

This trilateral request has multilateral meanings.

Bal: Strength without intelligence or discretion will make a person violent. In the Bhagavad Gita, Lord Krishna says, "Dadahmi budhi yogam", meaning, "whoever attaches himself to Me through devotion, I give intelligence." When we have strength, then we can do 'Karma Yoga'; a feeble person may be able to think but finds it difficult to execute his plans. 'Bal' also means 'Atma Bal or Mano Bal' which means mental strength to endure the ups and downs of life.

Buddhi: Intelligence which has no emotion is meaningless, rather it can be destructive. However, this does not take away from the importance of intelligence in our lives. It is said that if fate has designs to destroy someone, that person's intelligence is ruined first. Intelligence helps us in 'Gyana Yoga'.

Vidya: There is also a stream of thought that while 'Buddhi' can put us in 'Bandhan' (bondage), knowledge sets us free. Wisdom is an invaluable asset. Morari Bapu said that in his personal opinion, 'Vidya' is 'Bhakti Yoga'. This can be explained by citing Ramayana wherein Maya or illusion has been called 'Avidya' (lack of knowledge) and Bhakti, which is devotion, has been called 'Gyana' or knowledge/mystical science. A devotee may sing or dance but that is not madness. Instead, he is full of awareness. Such knowledge frees us from bodily ego or intellectual pride. We must interpret 'Vidya' here as spiritual knowledge.

It can be said of Hanuman that he is an ocean of all these three traits, as he has no dearth of strength, intelligence, or knowledge and this is amply demonstrated in various episodes of the Ramayana.

The search for Sita can be interpreted as Hanuman's search for the 'Aatma' or the soul.

In the Ramayana, Lord Hanuman uses 'Bal' to find Sita; he uses 'Buddhi' to bring together stones that have "Ra +M" written on them to build a bridge across the ocean to cross over to Lanka and he uses 'Vidya' to help provide salvation to the demons led by Ravan.

Describing the concept of 'Bhakti' or devotion further, Morari Bapu said that a devotee does not ask for 'Mukti' (liberation) rather he wants to keep his God 'Mukta' or free from any demands. A lover of God wants to accept the bondage of God, but he wants to keep his deity free and unobligated.

Facing Hard Times-Here Are 7 Things That Can Help You

When the going gets tough, the tough get going. But you are never alone; there are seven elements that can help you in your difficult patch.

Life is never a simple unchanging stillness; it is like a flowing river that twists and turns, springing over stones, rocks, and pebbles; gushing with all its might through cascades and whirlpools. We face highs and lows, successes, and failures, gains and losses. Amidst so many triumphs and troughs, how can we maintain a balanced mind and be in a state of steady emotional health?

Morari Bapu provided the answer from Dohavali Ramayana of Goswami Tulsidas during Day 16 of Hari Katha. This beautiful couplet can help us through our troubled times.

Tulsi asamay ke sakha dheeraj, dharma, vivek,

sahit, sahas, satya brat, Ram bharoso ek

(In troubled times, these are friends–patience, dharma (moral code), discretion, literature, courage, truth, and complete faith in God)

II Dohavali–447 II

Bapu began by pointing out that Tulsidas has used the word 'Asamay' (not your time) rather than 'Kusamay' (bad/hard times). This subtle nuance incorporates within it a positive outlook on life. He further added that the cogency of the couplet has found resonance in his own life and experience.

1. Dheeraj (patience): Patience is a great support when we face hardship. It gives us resilience and fortitude to bide time. In Bal Kaand of the Ramayana, it is noticed that only patience helped; whether it was Sati, who had to wait for 87000 years to reunite with her husband or Rati who waited for a full epoch till Dwapara Yuga to reunify with her partner Kama Deva. King Dasratha waited till old age before he was blessed with children.

2. Dharma (righteousness): Dharma is the righteous path and is explained by Morari Bapu as the practice of 'Truth, Love and Compassion'. In the Mahabharata, Pandavas faced severe plight and went through many trials. Even after the battle in Kurukshetra was over, they had to live with the loss of their own children and bear the mental agony that came with war. Eventually, their journey ended in the lofty Himalayas, where one by one they all perished. Only a dog remained till the end with Yudhisthir, and he entered heaven with him. The dog was believed to be none other than Dharma himself. Even in Ayodhya Kaand of the Ram Charita Manas, as preparations for coronation were underway, Ram was sent to exile dressed like an ascetic. But he bears all the ordeals–Ram tells Sumant in Sringaverpura:

"Sibi Dadhicha Harichandra naresa, sahe dharama hita koti kalesa."

(Sibi, Dadhicha and King Haricandra suffered untold hardships for the sake of virtue.)

II Ram Charita Manas–Ayodhya Kaand–95 II

3. Vivek (discretion): Prudence is what one gathers from Satsanga (holy congregations). But there is a further view about putting to use the good judgment that one gains. For example, there would be no use if one were to extract sugarcane juice but not bother to drink it! Similarly, we may have gained a lot of knowledge through the study of sacred texts, but it will be of little use if we don't apply what we have learnt to our lives. As per Hindu texts, when Harnakshasa had abducted Earth, God appeared in Varah avatar to rescue it. Similarly in the Ramayana in the episode related with Chitrakoot, when everyone was totally submerged in deep grief, at such a time it was Bharat's prudent judgment that salvaged the situation. In Aranya Kaand too there are several instances where you see the primacy of good judgment.

4. Sahit (literature): Literature could mean anything–not just shastras, mantras and sutras from scriptures but moral stories from folklore or popular writing. In Kishkindha Kaand there are many such sutras or learnings. Bapu then related one instance when India's first Prime Minister Jawaharlal Nehru missed a step while deplaning, author Ramdhari Singh Dinkar held out his hand to help him regain balance. When the former PM thanked him, Dinkar is believed to have stated that "*Jab rajniti ladkahadati hai to sahitya hi madat karta hai*" (When politics loses its balance, it is literature that comes to the rescue).

5. Sahas (courage). Sundar Kaand is full of instances of courage displayed by Lord Hanuman. If we were to evaluate the phase of Covid Lockdown, courage and endurance helped us through this prolonged period of self-isolation and many of us learnt to deal with aloneness.

6. Satya Vrat (pledge of honesty): We must hold on to truth in a steadfast manner, so much so that truth becomes our innate and intrinsic nature. We can learn from the doyens of India's freedom movement like Mahatma Gandhi and Vinobha Bhave. Darkness cannot be dispelled without light. Ram is truth incarnate and he dispels the darkness created by the demons, as seen in Lanka Kaand.

7. Ram Bharoso Ek (faith in God): Our complete faith and surrender must be in one place and there can be no scope for debate or argument there. Lord Shiva is symbolic of faith and when his wife Sati does not listen to his entreaties, Mahadev says, *'Hoi soi jo Ram rachi rakha, ko kare tarak badai sakha'* (that shall come to pass which is ordained, there is no point in getting into argument or debate over it). Uttar Kaand is symbolic of faith in God as seen through the example of Bhusundi who faced many tribulations but claimed that his unwavering mind remained immersed in the devotion of Ram like a fish remains submerged in water.

Morari Bapu ended the discourse by saying that though all seven canons were important, if he really had to choose only one, he would pick the last: 'Ram Bharoso Ek'.

How Many Types Of Friends Does God Have?

*I*n the Ramayana, Lord Ram who is considered an avatar had three *prime friends, besides another special relationship.*

God is a friend of all living beings as a principle. Though it is said that relationships always cause bondage, it is not the case when a saint or God is part of that relationship. Rather, such an association creates complete freedom or liberation.

In this context, Morari Bapu delved into the theme of friendship as witnessed in the Ramayana while speaking on Day 17 of Hari Katha. Lord Ram forges a friendship with three different people in the Ram Charita Manas. These people fall into different categories which are normally perceived in the world as 'Visheyi' (materialistic), 'Sadhak' (an aspirant learner on the spiritual path), and 'Siddh' (accomplished). However, Bapu adds that there is a fourth category called 'Shudh' (pure) who are very rare.

About the first three categories, the following became friends of the Lord:

1. Sugreev who belonged to the monkey community

2. Vibhishan who belonged to the demon community

3. Guharaj who belonged to the Nishad (fishermen) community

Examining the friendship of Sugreev, it seems he falls into the first category-'Visheyi' (materialistic), who is engrossed in sensual pleasures. He has many shortcomings; he is always fearful and even forgets to accomplish tasks for Lord Ram despite making promises. However, his biggest advantage is that he keeps Hanuman with him. This means, whatever may be our faults, if we have surrendered at the feet of a Sadaguru, the accomplished master will at some point help us forge a bond of friendship with God.

Vibhishan is slightly more elevated and can be called a 'Sadhak Sakha' (friend, who is a spiritual aspirant), said Morari Bapu. Lord Hanuman finds out in Sundar Kaand that Vibhishan chants the holy name, is a Vaishnav, has planted a Tulsi, and the name of Ram is painted in his house at various places. There is a 'Hari Mandir' (temple) just outside his house. These are all indications of a 'Sadhak'.

It can also be said that Vibhishan does not become a 'Badha' (impediment) to anyone. Bapu explained that 'Sadhak' is one who is not a 'Badhak' (creator of obstacles) for anyone by thought, words or actions. It is for this reason that Ravan also does not interrupt Vibhishan's spiritual pursuits and practices.

Nishadraj Guha, Bapu said, was 'Siddha' (spiritually accomplished). He lived on the banks of the Ganges; drank its water and bathed in it. He comes across as spiritually ripened. It can be said that considering his position in society-he belonged to an outcaste community-he may have suffered and endured much in life. What Ramkrishna Paramhamsa described as–'Chawal Siddh Ho Gaya'–the process of raw grain becoming edible by removing the husk and boiling.

When a spiritual master makes an aspirant undergo the process of removal of husk by beating it in a vessel and striking it and then boiling it, it is not 'Prahaar' (smashing/putting someone through hardship) but 'Prasad' (a gift). Guha has gone through this process in his life and has reached the stage of becoming like boiled rice which helps others in satiating hunger–meaning he has gained the capacity to help others.

Morari Bapu further elucidated that God gives rewards as per the spiritual stage of the aspirant. If one is 'Visheyi'–God gives 'Bhog' (material rewards). If one is a Sadhak, he will remove his 'Vishaad' (grief) and if one has reached the stage of becoming a 'Siddha', in the end, the person will be rewarded with bliss.

Bapu also recalled that once when he was asked to speak at the Ramkrishna Mission in Rajkot, he had stated that God gives a 'Visheyi'–'Shiksha' (teaching); 'Sadhak' is given 'Bhiksha' (alms), and 'Siddha' is given 'Dikhsa' (ordination).

Besides these three great friendships described in the Ramayana, there is a fourth friendship and that is with Lord Shiva. It is said of him–'Sevak Swami Sakha Siya Pi Ke' (He is the servant and master of the husband of Sita). He can be described as the 'Shudha-Buddha Sakha' (a friend who is completely pure and enlightened). Ram and Shiva are Hari-Har Swaroop, meaning they have become so close that they have actually become one.

Bapu said friendship is one such relationship in which we are completely transparent. We can talk about even those things that we are hesitant to reveal to our parents. It is not without reason that when in Srimad Bhagavatam the forms of 'Bhakti' (devotion) have been described 'Aatma Nivedinam' (revealing of personal thoughts) immediately follows after 'Sakhyam' (friendship).

It needs to be remembered that while relationships with mortals are limited to a lifetime and are finite, our relationship with God endures forever. Like the friendship between 'Ra' + 'M'-in the end, only the holy name remains.

Types Of Adversities
We Face In Our Lives

*T*here are three types of problems that we can face in our lives. Who doesn't face problems in life? We all have our own set of hurdles and each of us responds differently to the obstacle–some overcome it successfully, waiting for it to tide over patiently, while others succumb to anxiety and depression. Resilience as a trait in such trying times becomes the key. We can use worldly wisdom, seek help from friends or take spiritual recourse. Responding to a query from a listener during Day 18 of Hari Katha, Morari Bapu explained that there are three types of adversities that we can face in life.

Even in the Hanuman Chalisa, the word 'Sankat' (adversity) has come thrice. These lines are relevant even in contemporary times:

1. *Sankat se Hanuma chudave, mun kram bachan dhyan jo lave*

2. *Sankat kate mite sab pira jo sumaire Hanumant balbira*

3. *Pavan tanay Sankat haran mangal murti roop*

All three when translated in English loosely mean that the monkey god Hanuman can protect us from problems and hardships in life.

Speaking about the types of difficulties that one may face, Bapu elaborated about:

1. Pran Sankat: When there is a threat to our life.

2. Rashtra Sankat or Vishwa Sankat: When there is a national or global crisis.

3. Dharma Sankat: When there is a rise of unrighteousness and those who follow the principles of truth, love and compassion are challenged.

The question that arises next is about how one can overcome these problems. As suggested in the Hanuman Chalisa, by taking refuge in Hanuman or a perfect spiritual master like him, we can overcome impediments and phases that cause us to struggle.

However, our faith and commitment must be in one place. We must reach out, meditate upon, chant about, remember and keep in our hearts, the same divine element or person.

How Can We Tune Our Soul Into The Divine?

*H*ere is an interesting analogy between a transistor and the human soul. Both need fine–tuning to catch the right signal.

On Day 19 of Hari Katha, Morari Bapu recalled an incident from nearly five decades ago. Sometime between 1967 and 1970, he visited Odisha to see the good work being done by eye camps in remote villages. Not only was he deeply moved to witness extreme poverty, but he also remembered an interesting anecdote related by a Baul (wandering mendicant) of the area. The Baul drew a parallel between spiritual life and a radio transistor. That set Bapu thinking about why the radio of the human body and mind is unable to tune into divinity.

Morari Bapu first analysed five prime reasons why a normal radio does not pick signals from a station:

1. The radio may have some internal problem

2. It is not tuned into the correct station

3. The radio might have fallen and broken; maybe it's too old

4. Its battery might need recharging

5. Radio station program that was being broadcast might have concluded

Drawing an analogy with spiritual life, Bapu said most humans are unable to tune into God, unlike great saints, who are in sync with the celestial pulse of the universe.

There could be three characteristics in us that disrupt our signals due to our own internal problems.

1. Irsha: Jealousy/Envy
2. Ninda: Criticism of Others
3. Dwesh: Hatred for others

Bapu explained that while one can justify that some amount of lust is needed for procreation, greed/money is entailed because life can be lived only through material means, and some amount of anger may be required to instil discipline, but envy, criticism and hatred are not needed at all and serve no purpose.

Besides, we may need to change the direction of our soul's radio to set it in the right direction, meaning we need to know our real goal in life.

We must also tune-in at the right time i.e., not wait till we are too old and rather grasp the opportunity of spiritual advancement at an appropriate age.

Bapu finally summed up by saying that when a normal transistor does not work, we take it to a mechanic to fix it, similarly when our soul's radio needs mending, we must turn to a realized spiritual master for help.

Shiva Reveals Three Mystic Secrets In The Ramayana

*W*hat is the mystic meaning of Shankar Bhajan in Ram Charita Manas and what are the three secrets that are revealed by Lord Shiva?

The Ramayana is a sacred text with many intriguing secrets. The cryptic nuances and meanings in the scripture can be learnt only through an authoritative commentator or by divine inspiration. For example, the epic contains several dialogues including the conversation between Lord Ram and Sage Vishistha in Chitrakoot about the future of Ayodhya. Here, Sage Vishistha recommends to Lord Ram to first listen to his younger brother Bharat's plea and then refer to what is enjoined by 'sages, citizens, political heads, and the Vedas' before concluding on the issue.

Sage Vishistha says:

Bharata binaya sadar sunia karia bicharu bahori,

Karaba sadhumata lokamata nripanaya nigama nichori.

(Listen with attention to Bharata's humble submission and then think over it. Again, sifting the worldly point of view and the conclusions of holy men as well as of the political science and the Vedas, do what they enjoin upon you.)

II Ram Charita Manas–Ayodhya Kaand–Do 258 II

A deeply mystic meaning of 'Sadhumata' here actually points to Lord Shiva. According to Morari Bapu, who has been commenting on the Ramayana for nearly 60 years, Lord Shiva is a 'Param Sadhu' (greatest sage). What therefore could be Shiva's advice that is enigmatically embedded in various cantos of the Ramayana? Bapu explained the same on Day 20 of Hari Katha.

Bapu also turned his attention to an episode that takes place immediately after the rule of Lord Ram is established in Ayodhya on his return from exile. He then linked the two.

After taking over the reins and establishing Ram Rajya, Lord Ram puts forth his own views to the populace:

Aurau eka guputamata sabahi kahau kara jori,

Sankara bhajana bina nara bhagati na pavai mori.

(With joined palms I lay before you all another secret doctrine: without adoring Shankar (Lord Shiva) man cannot attain devotion to Me.)

II Ram Charita Manas-Uttar Kaand-Doha 45 II

This 'Guputamata' (secret) was disclosed out of love and remains pertinent for all periods of time. This proclamation of Lord Ram clearly states that a devotee gets the boon of devotion only through the grace of Lord Shiva.

For that we must do Shankar Bhajan (pray to Lord Shiva).

Ordinarily, one understands Shankar Bhajan as chanting mantras like 'Om Namah Shiva', meditating upon him, remembering him, singing Shiva Stotras or narrating his stories. But Bapu felt that this may not necessarily be the case. He explained that there are three experiences of Lord Shiva that we must incorporate into our lives with full faith. By doing so, we would be taking 'Sadhumata' and also doing Shankar Bhajan in reality.

Lord Shiva says:

1. *Hari Vyapak sarbatra samana, prem te pragat hohi mai jana*

   (For aught I know Sri Hari is present everywhere alike and is revealed only by love.)

   II Ram Charita Manas-Bal Kaand-Ch 185 II

   Lord Shiva says that God is omnipresent from the smallest grain of sand to the loftiest mountain and the mightiest ocean. God is all pervasive and is revealed with love. He also says:

   Uma kahau mai anubhav apna, Sat Hari bhajan jagat sab sapna

   (Uma, I tell you my own realization; the only thing real is the worship of Sri Rama, and the whole world is a dream.)

   II Ram Charita Manas–Aranya Kaand-Ch 39 A II

   Many say experience is greater than faith. But Bapu feels if we have been unable to experience divinity ourselves, then we must have faith in the person who has already experienced it.

2. Sunaho Sati tava nari subhau, sansaya asa na dharia ura kau.3.

   (Look here, Sati, you have the trait of a woman; you should never harbour such doubt in your mind.)

   II Ram Charita Manas-Bal Kaand-Ch 51 II

Shiva questions his consort that on one hand you say that I cannot ever lie and yet you are in doubt about what I am disclosing. Morari Bapu urged that once a devotee has truly felt his Guru to be supreme, no doubt should be allowed to sprout into the mind after that. It is necessary to first have full faith in a Sadaguru. But once that faith has been established, there should be no space or scope for mistrust. Like Ramkrishna Paramhamsa said–first fully circumambulate your Guru and examine him from all angles and only then repose firm faith in him.

3. Never do Guru Apraadh (commit sin against your Guru): Morari Bapu says a disciple must be very careful and attentive. A true Guru will drink poison if you make such a mistake, but Shiva cannot bear such a sin. Like the incident in Ujjain in the Ramayana when Bhusundi insults his Guru by not paying obeisance to him. Shiva did not forgive Bhusundi and immediately censured him with punishment.

Morari Bapu concluded by explaining a very significant line from the Ramayana. He said that there is one evidence in the Bal Kaand of Ram Charita Manas that substantiates what Shiva says is Sadhu Mat.

After Lord Shiva reveals that God is acquired through love, all gods present chant "Sadhu Sadhu"!

More bacana sab ke mun mana, "sadhu sadhu" kari brahma bakhana.4.

(My words found favour with all, and Brahma applauded me saying, "Well said, well said!–as by a Sage")

II Ram Charita Manas-Bal Kaand-Ch 185 II

Here too Lord Shiva being a Sadhu is affirmed.

The Difference Between Mun, Buddhi, Chit, Ahankar

These four terms—Mun, Buddhi, Chit, Ahankar—are often used in sacred scriptures. However, it is very difficult to understand the differentiators.

On Day 21 of Hari Katha, Morari Bapu recalled an incident from his childhood days. He was being mentored and tutored in spiritual studies and Ramayana by his grandfather Tribhuvana Das ji, whom Bapu also considers as his Sadaguru i.e., spiritual master. One day, Tribhuvana Das Dada asked Bapu whether he was able to follow the meaning of "Mun, Buddhi, Chit and Ahankar" (mind, intellect, psyche/conscience, and ego).

In the realm of spiritual studies, understanding the nuanced difference between these is vital but very difficult to comprehend. So, many years ago when Bapu was faced with a query from his grandfather, he had responded in the negative. But now, nearly six decades later, Bapu said he is touched by his grandfather's pure remembrance and inspired to respond.

His grandfather Tribhuvana Das ji had explained something to this effect:

1. *Mun kayam abhaav vadi hota hai:* Mun or the Mind always presents the picture of deprivation. However much a

person may receive, the mind always pushes a person to feel that it is not enough. The more one gets, the more one wants. Whether it is sensual pleasures, wealth or various other types of desires, the mind never lets us feel that we have reached a point of saturation.

2. *Buddhi prabhav vadi hoti hai:* The intellect always wants to impress others; create a favourable or powerful impact on others. A person of high intelligence feels deep remorse if he is unable to influence or sway those around him or make a mark for himself.

3. *Chit swabhav vadi hota hai:* Our conscience or psyche carries all the hallmarks of our personal nature. It travels with us, birth after birth, through several lifetimes carrying profound stamps of our personal traits–whether we are easily provoked into anger, attracted by material gains or are highly aware and learned.

4. *Ahankar durbhav vadi hota hai*–Ego never lets us live in peace with others. It always causes ill will against others because our ego cannot see circumstances favouring others. And due to ill will, we speak ill of others. This is a major ailment.

Bapu feels that more than enjoying the physical company of a Guru, it is best for the devotee to stay close to the thoughts of his spiritual master. One must live in constant remembrance of his Guru, his words, thoughts, and characteristics, for these will help a disciple, physical distance notwithstanding.

Learning From Saint Kabir's Internal And External Journey

*K*abir is one of the most important saints of the Bhakti Movement in India. Here is a look at the mission of his life extraordinaire.

One of the greatest stars in the Indian spiritual firmament has been saint Kabir. A 15th century mystic poet, his thoughts and words were revolutionary for his times, and his beliefs put him at odds with the established clergy which was trapped in dogma and orthodox practices. Kabir, whose birth remains a mystery, was unlettered, yet his rustic words brought out the truth in the most genuine way and have touched the hearts of millions. His couplets have been recorded in the Guru Granth Sahib as well. Speaking on Day 23 of Hari Katha, Morari Bapu picked the topic of Kabir and explained his philosophy.

KRANTIKARI, BHRANTIHARI AND SHANTIKARI

Morari Bapu described this great sage from Kashi as a Krantikari (revolutionary), Bhrantihari (remover of false beliefs), and Shantikari (someone who spreads peace).

Bapu explained that he felt Kabir was revolutionary as he constantly took a different route than the well-trodden path. And because he was a fully realized soul, he had the courage to question and contest superstitions, defy traditional rituals which were being blindly followed, and also challenge miracles and fallacies.

Kabir's lifelong mission was to free people from misconceptions related to religion and that is precisely what made him a great spiritual doyen.

As a prominent figure in the Bhakti movement, his words provided solace and peace. That is why he can be called 'Shantikari'. Bapu felt that the characteristics found in a realized soul as per Sufis, Zen masters, Bauls and Margi Sadhus were all present in him.

The fact is that he was a triumvirate of three radically different qualities.

What must also be appreciated is that whenever we suffer from a 'Bhranti' (delusion), it is mostly an external attribute like in the case of Sati in Ramayana who saw Lord Ram roaming in the jungles looking for Sita and became deluded. 'Kranti'(revolution) takes place by listening to the inspiring words of a fully realized spiritual master. His words are like rays of the sun that dispel all darkness of delusion. And 'Shanti' or peace can be experienced only inside us; it is an internal feeling.

AN INTERNAL AND EXTERNAL JOURNEY

Kabir's journey was both internal and external. An external journey is required for cleanliness and an internal journey is a must to obtain purity.

Because there was so much pollution in the external world through the spread of fallacies and incorrect beliefs and totems, Kabir undertook the external journey to cleanse these.

But on a personal level, he undertook an internal journey, which filled him with spiritual purity.

A spiritual master is one whose birth, birthplace, parents etc. are of little consequence. It is difficult to comment upon his life, as his actions are full of enigmas. How he leaves the world is also a mystery.

But the one whose birth and life do not cause pain to anyone, such a person is in the true sense a realized soul, Bapu said.

There are many tales related to the birth and death of Kabir- in fact there is no conclusive narrative on these. His actions in his lifetime can also confuse an ordinary person. For example, it is a traditional belief that whatever may be an account of our karmas, a soul achieves Nirvana if the person passes away in the holy city of Varanasi. And if death takes place in Maghar, then all merits earned during a lifetime vanish.

Kabir did just the opposite-he lived all his life in Kashi and in old age, as he neared his end, he moved to Maghar. The saint wanted to send out a message that Nirvana is not merely limited to a particular geographical location or 'Bhoomi', but it has everything to do with 'Bhoomika' or eligibility earned through actions.

When he passed away, his Hindu and Muslim followers claimed his body for last rites and burial as per their respective religious faiths. Kabir resolved the quandary because when the sheet was lifted from his body, there were only flowers. People of both faiths divided them and accorded them last rites.

In this way, though Kabir showcased both internal and external journeys for providing cleanliness in the societal belief systems and experiencing purity on the inside, importantly, his message was to keep making that journey.

Lord Krishna On Traits Of A Person Who Has Achieved Divinity

*L*ord Krishna has delineated specific characteristics in a person who has achieved the divine light.

In the spiritual stream, there is great value associated with a person who is considered 'Realized'. A self-realized soul, as described in the Bhagavad Gita, is supposed to have achieved the 'Self' or the inner light. He understands divinity and has become a part of the Supersoul. Taking up the issue of the traits displayed by a person who has achieved such lofty spiritual heights, Morari Bapu, revealed Sri Krishna's thoughts on the subject on Day 24 of Hari Katha.

Bapu revealed that Lord Krishna has emphasized upon four major characteristics that should be in a person who can be recognized as 'Bhagvat Prapt' or someone who has achieved divinity.

Sri Krishna says a person who has the following qualities has achieved me:

1. Who is satisfied by Gyana (knowledge) and Vigyana (divine science): Human beings are always searching for knowledge. We need to reach a stage where we feel we are satisfied with what we know. 'Gyana' is 'Yoga' (in this context discipline) while 'Vigyana' is 'Prayoga' (experiment). That is why when someone asked Bapu

about what the aim of life was, he recommended that we set aside such questions and just be. And be satisfied.

2. One who is Kutastha (a person established in the highest position). Such a person is free from all vices, weaknesses, and faults. He is full of 'Vivek yukta stithi' i.e., correct discrimination. As per Vinobha Bhave, such a person should be 'Nirbhaya' (fearless), 'Nishpaksha' (impartial) and 'Nirvair' (free from animosity). Morari Bapu said that it follows that a person can only be fearless when he is honest. It is impossible to be fearless if one is not speaking the truth. Impartiality is not possible without compassion, and lack of animosity is achieved only through love in the heart.

3. Jitendriya (a master of his senses): He is a person who has won over his senses naturally. Morari Bapu felt that it is preferable to say that someone has filled the five senses with discretion and uses prudence in seeing, listening, touching, speaking, tasting, and smelling rather than saying he has "won over the senses".

4. Ucchate (evenness of mind): A person who has achieved evenness of mind and sees soil, gold, and stone with the same eye. To him all three are the same. All three are obtained from the earth as is a Sadhu (saint). Soil or dust becomes special when it touches the feet of a Divine Master. Such a person either feels the three elements are the same or simply rises above them.

What Is The Ultimate Quality Of Spiritual Surrender?

*T*he *celebrated stanzas called 'Ashrey Ke Pad' of the famous saint–poet Surdas continue to hold the benchmark for ultimate spiritual surrender.*

Shri Vallabhacharya established the 'Pushti Marg' in the Hindu system of worship. In this tradition, there is importance of 'Ashta Sakhas' or eight friends including the well-known saint Surdas, whose 'Ashrey Ke Pad', stanzas of surrender to his Guru are extremely popular and regularly recited. These effuse of emotion and are a testimony to his complete refuge in his Guru. On Day 25 of Hari Katha, Morari Bapu said that by understanding the subtleties of these stanzas, one comprehends the 'nature of surrender' to a Realized Master.

In the famous 'Ashrey Ka Pad' by Surdas is written:

Bharoso, Drud In Charan Kairo

I have unwavering and absolute faith in the feet of my spiritual guru Sri Vallabha.

Sri Vallabh Nakh Chandra Chhata Bin, Sab Jag Mahi Andhero

Without whose holy presence and light of toenail, I find darkness in the whole world.

Sadhan Aur Nahi Ya Kali Main, Jaso Hot Nivero

In the darkest age of Kali yuga (epoch) what other means do I have except his refuge.

Sur Kaha Kahe, Vivadha Andhero, Bina Mol Ke Chero

So says Surdas, that I am blind in two ways. I am visually impaired and can't see the world and secondly, I cannot see the difference between God, Sri Nath ji and Sri Vallabh, the Guru to whom I offer my unconditional servitude.

One must examine these valuable words closely to understand the underlying sentiment in them. When Surdas uses the word 'Charanan Kero' it is a testament of his unwavering faith in these 'particular feet'-of his Guru-and the use of the words 'In Charanan' means 'these feet and no other'.

It is not that he is negating the value of other revered feet, it is only evidence of his own commitment to only one place. Generally, feet are symbolic of movement, gait, and speed. But in this stanza, Surdas indicates that these are fixed-the divine feet can reach numerous places without actually moving-as indicated in the Ramayana-'Binu Padu Chale' (God can reach anywhere without physical feet). Only divine feet have this ability as they rush to the rescue of those who have taken refuge in them.

Surdas feels Mahaprabhu's feet are beautiful, and these are the single destination for his faith. All his wandering has seized. Morari Bapu explained, "Paduka (Guru's sandals) and the feet of a spiritual master are our security and motivator, as displayed in the case of Bharat in the Ramayana."

Surdas feels his surrender in the feet of Vallabhacharya is as resolute as his Guru's feet. Morari Bapu explained that spiritual surrender or 'Sharangati' can be of 3-4 types:

1. Sharirik Sharnagati (bodily refuge): Sometimes our surrender is only limited to the physical boundary of a Guru. Like bowing at the feet of an Acharya and providing service for his comfort.

2. Vachik Sharnagati (faith in a Guru's words): For example, we say–'Sri Ram Dutam Sharanam Prapade' for Hanuman. We declare our surrender by chanting it. Or like Rukmini expressed her surrender in a letter to Krishna saying she has heard his praise. This sanctuary is subtler than the 'Bodily Refuge' mentioned above.

3. Mansik Sharnagati (mental surrender): Deeper still is the surrender where a devotee does not press to be physically close to his Lord or even attempts to touch his feet. He remembers his spiritual master fondly from a distance and is satisfied.

4. Aatmik Sharnagati (submission to his soul): This is the subtlest form of refuge out of the four. Here, one feels that whatever the Guru desires is the ultimate verdict for him. There is no scope of ifs and buts in it.

Bapu feels that Bharosa (belief) is the outcome of the marriage of Shraddha (devotion) and Vishwas (faith).

All three–belief, devotion and faith are great virtues, but these need to be steadfast. Unfortunately, we lose faith easily and sometimes even blame the person at whose feet we have surrendered.

In worldly love, there is ardor, passion, disagreements, and patch ups. But the love for your Guru should be tenacious and unwavering; never being disturbed by the ripples of events or highs and lows of one's life.

Bapu said, a disciple needs to make a choice, "Either he leaves the outcome of all events to his Guru, or he should leave his Guru." There can be no middle way in this.

Surdas says Vallabhacharya's feet are 'Achalit'-meaning these are firmly grounded. And so is his faith. He feels that the toenail of his Guru's feet is the source of the light of his life, and, for him, the rest of the world seems encompassed in darkness. His usage of the term "submerged in darkness" is an acknowledgement and expression of his complete humility and ineptitude. His Guru is his anchor.

Surdas says: *Sri Vallabh Nakh Chandra Chhata Binu Sab Jag Mahe Andhero*

What is noteworthy is that Surdas is talking about the toenail providing light when he himself is visually impaired. Clearly, the poet-saint could sense and discern the supreme power without having eyesight. What he is possibly also referring to is the internal blindness of the world which is experiencing delusion and indulges in vices like criticism, avarice, anger, lust, malice, and hatred of others.

Who will guide such a person except a Realized Master in whom one has absolute faith! Like a caretaker navigates the way for a blind man, so does a Guru for a committed disciple who seeks nothing from his Master.

Morari Bapu advocated that one must therefore continuously remember his Guru, sing the praises of divine and listen to

His supreme qualities, as espoused by Goswami Tulsidas in the same vein at the conclusion of the Ram Charita Manas as well.

Five Milestones Of Self-Realization

From beholding a Guru to finding absolute bliss–what are the stages of a spiritual journey?

It is often discussed, sometimes pondered over and rarely understood–the many steps of a spiritual journey from finding and beholding a true Guru to the stage of self-realization and bliss.

A beautiful stanza written by Guru Arjan Dev (the 5th Guru of the Sikhs) under the pseudonym of 'Nanak' in the Guru Granth Sahib brilliantly illustrates the journey. The verse written in Raga Saarang on page 1218 of the Guru Granth Sahib was explained by Morari Bapu on Day 26 of Hari Katha.

The canto enlists 5 steps:

1. *Utari Gayo Mere Mann Ka Sansha Jab Te Darshan Paya (1)*

   The first line says, "O my Lord and Master, I have come to your sanctuary. The anxiety of my mind departed when I gazed upon the blessed vision of yours."

   Whatever delusion and darkness that exists in us is destroyed by the mere sight of a Guru or after we have completely surrendered at the feet of a spiritual master. Darshan is a uniquely Indian concept. It is to behold a vision, in this case of a Sadaguru. Bapu explained, "Even in Bhagavad Gita, God says that once a person calls out to me and takes refuge in me, I make that person fearless."

This is the first fruit of coming into the compass of a true Spiritual Master. Sometimes, not even a word is exchanged; the mere presence of a realized soul has such an impact.

In the Ramayana, Garuda says to Bhusundi:

Dekhi param pavan tava asram, gayau moha samsaya nana bhrama

(At the very sight of your most holy hermitage, my infatuation, doubt, and many misconceptions have been removed.)

II Ram Charit Manas–Uttar Kaand–64 II

2. *Anbolat Meri Birthaa Jaani Apna Naam Japaya*

Ramayana exponent Morari Bapu explained that in the second stage a devotee starts feeling like this, "You know my condition, without my speaking. You inspire me to chant the Holy Name."

A true master is omniscient. He knows the state and the problems of a devotee without these being openly expressed. A Guru knows how to untangle the knots that are impeding a disciple.

The Master next gives the disciple the ability to chant the Holy Name. We ourselves can make only very limited progress. It is the divine push from a realized soul that helps us immerse in the 'Name of God', which removes our agony.

3. *Dukh Naathey Sukh Sahaj Samaye Anand Anand Gun Gaya*
    (1)

"My pains are gone, and I am absorbed in peace, poise and bliss, singing Your Glorious Praises."–As our Jap (chanting) increases, our reasons for our grievances and sorrows disappear just like frogs jump out of a pond when a buffalo enters.

As our pain points are eased, we feel a new sense of joy and happiness. Being in 'Bliss' is our 'Mool Swabhav' (natural condition), as per Morari Bapu. We are re-established in that state.

The same is referenced in the Ramayana:

Isvara ansa jiva abinasi, chetan amala sahaja sukha rasi.1

(The soul is a particle of the Divinity, immortal, conscious, untainted by Maya or Illusion and blissful by nature.)

II Ram Charita Manas–Uttar Kaand–117 (A) II

Bapu then took the reference of Bhagavad Gita about– 'who is truly happy?'

Saknotihava yah sodhum prak sarira–vimoksanat

Kama–krodhabhavam vegam sa yuktah sa sukhi narah

II Bhagavad Gita–Chapter 5–Verse 23 II

Krishna tells Arjuna a person who before his death has managed to control the torrential force of lust and anger and remains balanced always, he is truly happy.

4. *Baah Pakad Kad Leenay Apne Griha Andh Koop Te Maya*

"Taking me by the arm, You lifted me up, out of the deep dark pit of household and Maya," a devotee is filled with such gratitude.

'Andh Koop' is inspired from the thoughts in the Upanishads wherein such a well (as was found in olden time villages) was so deep that people got dizzy just looking inside from the edges; a fall meant certain death.

All our materialistic chores are at the end only entanglements. And a person is so entrenched in such daily tasks that he feels he is unable to retrieve himself from the situation. One is so immersed in matters of finance, earnings, running a household and engaging with family members that there is scant time left for spiritual contemplation.

It is in such situation that a Guru comes to our rescue and pulls us of the scenario-this does not mean adopting asceticism but the ability to look beyond the material world and find time for devotional pursuits.

5. *Kaho Nanak Guru Bandhan Kaate Bichhurat Aan Milaya (2)*

"Says Nanak, the Guru has broken my bonds, and ended my separation; He has united me with God."

This is the final stage. After having traversed the journey from finding and beholding a guru to his understanding of our unsaid distress to the dispelling of grief and chanting of the holy name and enjoying blissful moments to escaping the web of the material world, a devotee finally finds that all bonds are broken, and his soul is liberated, and he is situated in Realization.

Five Ways On How Mira Won Over Krishna

*A*n *avant garde name in the Bhakti movement is that of Mirabai of Rajasthan. What was the nature of her devotion which is considered an epitome of divine adoration?*

Mirabai, the famous queen and saint from Rajasthan whose passion and devotion for Krishna epitomized the concept of Bhakti, has been celebrated in India in myriad forms. To date, we sing bhajans that were penned by her and organize dance and drama programs based on her sonnets and her life. She has been depicted on celluloid time and again and has been the subject of much examination in many books. There is both mystery and mysticism surrounding her persona.

Born into royalty, she was married at a young age to Bhoj Raj, the crown prince of Mewar. She was reluctant to be betrothed for her mind and soul were already committed to Nandalal of Gokul-Krishna. Widowed within five years of marriage and then persecuted by her brother-in-law, she wanders around engrossed in her devotional longing. Eventually, her life comes to an end at the Dwarka temple where she immerses herself in the idol.

Commenting on the enigmatic life of Mirabai, Morari Bapu, on Day 27 of Hari Katha recalled his childhood days. The

Ram ji temple of his village Talgajarda, where he worshiped, had a deity of Krishna. The Krishna idol, on each side, had statues of two women; the first was Mirabai and the other Radha.

About Mirabai, Bapu felt that love is the main foundation of her devotion. She is deeply absorbed in the ardor of Krishna and her devotional songs have the word 'Prem or Preeti', as a recurrent theme. The saint from Medta has been called 'Prem Diwani' or one who is ecstatic in divine fervour. She sings, "*Toso Preet Tod Krishna Kaun Sang Jodu.*" (With whom can I conjoin in a relationship other than you). For Mira, there is no alternative! In another couplet she says, "*Jo Main Janti Preeti Kiye Dukh Hoi.*" (If only I knew about how much love hurts...).

Further, Morari Bapu said, her devotion to Krishna appears to be 5-dimensional and goes through three stages–Raag (attachment) to Anurag (affection) and Vairag (detachment). Elaborating on the five dimensions, Bapu explains that her love can be compared with a vine:

- Firstly, her love is the seed of that creeper.

- The buds on the vine are her songs–the many couplets she wrote and rendered.

- The flowers, which swing with the wind, are her dances– '*Ghungroo bandh Mira Nachi*' describes how she too swayed with her music.

- The next stage is for the flowers to become an offering at Krishna's feet. Mira herself is the flower at Krishna's feet. She completely surrenders to him in mind, body, senses, and soul. She reaches a stage where she immerses herself in Krishna's idol in Dwarka. Many intellectuals have raised questions about this incident, but the immersion of one's entity and identity into another is the *'Puma samparpan aur sharnagati'* (epitome of surrender).

- The fifth and last dimension is the eternal, never effacing fragrance–Mirabai is an everlasting fragrance, which you cannot touch but only sense. The scent of her devotion spread far and wide and has sustained through the centuries.

Five Impediments On The Spiritual Path And Three Ways To Overcome Them

Apursuer of the spiritual path must brace for obstacles. But with faith, these can be overcome.

One of the most intriguing but also intimidating parts of a spiritual journey is the hurdles that appear. An aspirant finds that while he or she intensifies devotional pursuits, more often than not, the person fails again and again, owing to a multitude of causes. This sentiment was expressed in a letter to Morari Bapu on Day 29 of Hari Katha. The writer from Jabalpur asked about the impediments that present themselves as we make progress in the Bhautik (material), Daivik (that of demi-gods) and Aadhyatmik (spiritual) orbit.

Difficulties in the material world can be manifold. These could be karmic, an outcome of our past actions; at other times these would be owing to our loss of Vivek or power of discretion. Factors beyond our control can also come into play-natural disasters such as earthquakes, floods, or outbreak of diseases like Covid-19. It is under these circumstances, when we find ourselves totally helpless, that our faith is tested.

Kathopanishad says that if one is characterless, wallowing in bad habits, always restless and chasing endless desires, and whose Chit (psyche) is constantly disturbed or deflected, such a person, however rich or intelligent cannot achieve self-realization.

Morari Bapu elucidated that while the impediments in worldly quests are ad hoc and can come at any point, hindrances in the spiritual course are more defined and sequential. Sage Ramana Maharishi also corroborated the thought that the spiritual journey is more definitive in its progression, much like a train that stops at pre-defined stations for fixed durations. An analogy of a train halting for a longer time at a major station is akin to a larger obstacle.

Citing the Ram Charita Manas, Morari Bapu gave examples of these spiritual obstructions by drawing a parallel with Bharat's journey from Ayodhya to Chitrakoot. Queen Kaikeyi's son, Bharat, discovers that Lord Ram has been sent to exile for 14 years owing to a boon his mother had asked of King Dasratha. Shocked and distressed, he goes to Chitrakoot to persuade Lord Ram to return to Ayodhya.

1. Firstly, Bharat vows to travel barefoot to Chitrakoot because Lord Ram, along with Sita and Lakshman, too was without a vehicle. So, he begins walking, and seeing him do so, the people of Ayodhya also discard their vehicles. He is then persuaded by Queen Kaushalya to use a chariot in the interest of Ayodhya's subjects, who are not in a condition to make the journey on foot. Eventually, Bharat agrees and mounts a vehicle. Bapu says, similarly, a disciple who makes his resolve public is usually forced to abandon it. So, it is best not to be very vocal about one's spiritual practices.

2. Next, when Guharaj finds out that Bharat is coming into the forest and is accompanied by hordes of people, he misunderstands Bharat's intentions. Nishadraj feels that Bharat might be wanting to eliminate Ram, and thus becomes determined to take on Ayodhya's army in a battle along with his community's legion. So much so that Guharaj and his men are even willing to give up their lives, but finally the misunderstanding is cleared, and the tribal king rather becomes a guiding force in Bharat's excursion. In the same way, society misunderstands a devotee and opposes him, but if one's intentions are pure and selfless, these misapprehensions dissipate.

3. Thirdly, Sage Bharadwaj of Prayagraj tests Bharat by extending luxurious comforts, but Bharat remains unentangled. A devotee is tested by a Saint, just like Bharat or even Parvati who is tested by Sanat Kumars. One should therefore remain devoted to the spiritual cause and be indifferent to worldly pleasures.

4. Fourthly, Indra and other deities create obstacles for Bharat. But the guru of demigods, Brihaspati, admonishes them and tells them to mend their thinking.

5. Finally, as Bharat nears his destination, his brother Lakshman too misreads him. Lakshman, who had accompanied Ram to the jungle, felt Bharat had ill intentions, or else he would not have been accompanied by the army. Lakshman goes to the extent of wanting to kill him on the battlefield. But Lord Ram steps in and speaks in favour of Bharat. When one comes close to God, some family members will turn against the person. Eventually, like Lakshman, family members realize their

mistake and shower affection on the spiritual aspirant instead.

Considering that these hindrances are daunting, we can strive to overcome them through three main factors:

1. *Akhand and Abhed Shradha*-One needs to remain steadfast and resolute in one's purpose and devotion.

2. *Sadhu Sangh*-The company of saints and guidance go a long way in helping a disciple.

3. *Prabhu Naam Priyata*-Love for the holy name and constantly chanting it.

Morari Bapu said that one cannot wish away obstacles and a traveller on the spiritual path must brace for them. Eventually, for a sincere devotee, these impediments become enablers. The narrator of Ram Charita Manas also explained that in spirituality, after we complete our passage, we discover that the destination was actually the starting point. But to truly realize this, we need to make the full voyage.

One must therefore try and remain on the right path. However, if one fails, then a devotee should approach a bona fide master. Like Arjun, who is unable to gain composure in Kurukshetra, turns to Krishna to guide him. And though Krishna explains the transcendental philosophy in detail, eventually Krishna tells Arjun to give up everything and turn to Him alone:

Sarva-Dharmān Parityajya Mām Ekaṁ Śharaṇaṁ Vraja

(Abandon all varieties of dharmas and simply surrender unto me alone).

II Bhagavad Gita-Chapter 18-Verse 66 II

Hurdles Faced By Hanuman And Lord Ram

Three characters of Ramayana faced a total of 18 impediments–what do these signify and what lessons do they hold?

Prasthānatrayī is a uniquely Indic concept that denotes three sources, more particularly three canonical texts of theology. World famous exponent of Ram Katha, Morari Bapu, had once during a Hanuman Jayanti programme called Sant (saint), Hanumant (Lord Hanuman) and Bhagvant (God) as Prasthānatrayī. However, on Day 30 of Hari Katha, viewers urged Bapu to explain the literal and root meaning of the term. Morari Bapu explained that Prasthānatrayī as a construct was introduced by Adi Shankaracharya who used it to refer to the Brahmasutras, Upanishads and the Bhagavad Gita.

Giving Prasthānatrayī a new dimension in reference to the Ram Charita Manas, Bapu, talked about three journeys–one undertaken by a Sant (in this case Bharat), Hanumant and also Bhagvant i.e., Lord Ram. Bharat undertook an excursion from Ayodhya to Chitrakoot, Hanuman travelled from Kishkindha to Trikut (Lanka), and Lord Ram voyaged several times, first from Ayodhya to Chitrakoot on foot and then from Panchavati to Kishkindha on Hanuman's back, from

Rameswaram to Lanka on a Setu (bridge) and in the battlefield of Lanka on Indra's chariot.

Morari Bapu explored the impediments that the three main protagonists of the Ramayana face. Bharat, who is considered a saint, had to overcome 5 obstacles. Lord Hanuman had to tackle 6 hurdles and Lord Ram had to prevail over 7 hindrances. Taken together the three had to surmount 18 challenges.

As far as Bharat's journey is concerned, Morari Bapu had dealt with the subject at length on Day 29 of Hari Katha (please refer to Chapter 27). So, he next picked the topic of Hanuman's journey and explained it. Interestingly, in the venture to find Sita, the search party is headed by Bali's son Angad and guided by Jamvant. Hanuman is, in fact, the last person in the troupe. Yet, he is the one who makes a success of the expedition which was not an easy one:

1. Firstly, the band is lost deep in a jungle with only few days left for the month to complete, the stipulated time assigned for Sita's search, but there is yet no sign of her. Everyone in the party is thirsty, famished and on the verge of dying. At this stage, Hanuman locates Swayamprabha's cave, which proves to be a lifeline for them as they get water, nourishment, and direction. In this case, the first obstacle is hunger and thirst-the dharmas of Pran (lifeforce). Just like birth and death are dharmas of the body, and joy and distress are dharmas of the mind.

2. Next, the search party finds itself on the seashore. There, Sampati, who is Jamvant's brother, is hungry for many days and wants to feed on them. But due to their

mission's association with Lord Ram and Jamvant, a change of heart occurs in Sampati. Eventually, the hunter becomes the saviour and also their guide. If one's journey is of truth, love, and compassion, then obstacles turn into facilitators.

3. Mainak Hill was a golden hill which offers Hanuman a breather. Mainak Hill innately implies the allure of comfort and luxury. A devotee generally becomes indolent in his journey. As we seek to find Bhakti (devotion), Shakti (inner power) and Shanti (peace), laziness and temptations of luxury are impediments.

4. Sursa was sent by demigods to test Hanuman's strength, intelligence, and power of discretion. She finds Hanuman is an ace in all three and blesses him to succeed in his mission.

5. Sinhika, who is the mother of Rahu, catches shadows of those flying in the sky above her and makes them her prey. Hanuman identifies and slays her immediately.

6. Lankini, the guard of the kingdom of Lanka, stops Lord Hanuman at the entrance, but is quickly overwhelmed by him. She then welcomes him to enter the city and complete his mission.

Morari Bapu then moved to Lord Ram's expedition and the seven obstacles that he faced. Number seven is very significant in the Ramayana; there are seven cantos of Ram Charita Manas and seven couplets of Mangalacharan (introductory salutations) and seven questions that Garuda asked of the crow saint Bhusundi nearing the conclusion of the epic. Bapu explained that when we examine the obstructions faced by the prince of Ayodhya, we must first appreciate that Lord Ram is independent of Karma. In fact, anyone who is not covetous or does not aspire for the fruits of Karma, remains unbound by it.

It is in the light of this understanding that we should view these seven obstacles:

1. Firstly, when Lord Ram and Lakshman leave with Sage Vishwamitra, the first obstacle is Tadaka, the fierce demoness who attacks them. With a single shaft, Lord Ram takes her life and provides her with Nirvana.

2. Next, her sons Maricha and Subahu create blockades in Sage Vishwamitra's yagna. With a fire arrow, Lord Ram eliminates Subahu, while with a headless shaft, he throws Maricha miles away beyond the seashore, from where he would later be granted Nirvana.

3. After Ram is betrothed to Sita by dispensing Lord Shiva's bow, he is confronted by an enraged Parshuram. He too is subdued after a prolonged discourse.

4. Then after some time, in Panchavati, Shupnakha, the sister of Ravan, confronts Lord Ram and tries to lure him. But she is taught a lesson and sent back to Ravan as a provocation.

5. Shupnakha then instigates demons Khar and Dushan to avenge her humiliation. Khar and Dushan are considered Raag (attachment) and Dwesh (hatred); they are both overcome in a battle by Lord Ram singlehandedly.

6. In search for Sita, Lord Ram is faced by the Kabandha, who had become a demon due to a curse. Lord Ram kills him and also frees him of the terrible spell.

7. Finally, Ram exterminates Ravan, who is considered Jad (gross element) and provides him salvation as well.

Morari Bapu through examples of Lord Hanuman and Lord Ram, explained that a spiritual aspirant should not be deterred by small or big problems. With resilience, these can be overcome.

If a devotee finds that he is getting overwhelmed by hindrances on the spiritual path, then there are two other scaffolds that he can seek.

Morari Bapu said his grandfather, Tribhuvana Das ji, used to often say "Gurudev Samarth". A bonafide master can help us, just like Bharat helped the entire population of Ayodhya to make the journey to Chitrakoot.

We too can seek refuge in the Prasthānatrayī of Sant, Hanumant or Bhagvant to help us cross hurdles in our spiritual quest. Else we can take recourse of the 18 Manke Ka Berkha (by chanting the holy name on 18-beaded rosary) to trounce these 18 obstacles.

Exploring The Nature Of True Love!

*O*ur primeval and most basic instinct since life first breathed on earth is that of love. What are its most abiding and core qualities?

The image of Narad Muni immediately conjures up a very interesting persona in front of our eyes. A sworn bachelor, he is the eternally travelling sage singing the praises of Lord Vishnu and narrating enlightening fables. Narad is supposed to have been born out of the mind of Brahma, the creator of the world and the entire universe. His roving is epic as he pierces through many skies and celestial planets, participating in seminal events across realms. Sage Narad makes an appearance in several epics like the Ramayana and the Mahabharata as also in many Puranas, which are all holy texts.

Talking on the subject of Narad on Day 31 of Hari Katha during Lockdown, Morari Bapu, informed that in the tenth chapter of the Bhagavad Gita, known as the Vibhuti Yoga, where Lord Krishna names his several opulence, Narad is mentioned as one of his powerful manifestations.

Asvatthah Sarva–Vrksanam Devarsinam Cha Naradh
Gandharvanam Chitrarathah Siddhanam Kapilo Munih

Of all trees I am the holy fig tree (Peepul), and amongst sages and demigods, I am Narad. Of the singers of the gods

(Gandharvas), I am Chitraratha, and among perfected beings I am the sage Kapila.

II Bhagavad Gita–Chapter 10–Verse 26 II

Narad is mentioned in the Ramayana as well. To the surprise of his consort Parvati, Lord Shiva narrates how Lord Ram once took avatar on earth due to a curse put on him by Narad.

Narad srapa dinha eka bara, kalapa eka tehi lagi avatara

Girija chakita bhai suni bani, Narad Vishnu bhagata puni gyani.3.

(On one occasion Narad cursed the Lord; this served as an excuse for His birth in one particular epoch. Girija was taken aback to hear these words and said, "Narad is a votary of God Vishnu and an enlightened soul too.")

II Ram Charita Manas–Bal Kaand 124 A II

Morari Bapu informed that it is believed that the primeval creator, Astitva (God), has an Antahkaran (inner conscience) comprising Mun (mind), Buddhi (intelligence), Chit (psyche), and Ahankar (ego), and that Narad is considered God's 'Mun'.

One of the great contributions of Narad Muni is his famous Bhakti Sutras. His commentary on devotion contains 84 tenets that are considered the ultimate maxims of love.

As per Morari Bapu, the six characteristics of love mentioned by Narad are undisputed and unparalleled:

1. Guna Rahitam (without specific characteristics): Love is without specific shape or property. We can make a sculpture of the lover but not that of love. It is formless. In Indian philosophy, Gunas are of three types–Satvo

(mode of goodness), Rajo (mode of passion), Tamo (mode of ignorance). Love also has three levels–Sthool Prem which is the most basic love is related to the physical aspect, where the body is central to it. This stage is primarily related to Tamo Guna. The aspect that has Shringaar (adornments), Adaiye (style and coquetry), and Ishare (gestures), these are related with Rajo Guna. In Satvo Guna, the heart is at the centre of love. Love that is free from all these three modes is supreme love–where there is no mind, intelligence, psyche, or ego. This is the love of the soul. Narad is talking about love of the soul, which is a deeply internal journey.

2. Kamna Rahitam (without desire): This means love and devotion that are without any expectation of return. There is no desire to get anything for the love which we have for the other person. True love does not have any expectations; rather the person surrenders himself or herself to the other.

3. Pratikshan Vardhamana (growing every moment): Normally, one becomes bored or wearies due to excessive interaction with the person one loves; everyone wants space. Real love never fatigues; it grows with each moment.

4. Avichinnam (unbroken): True love is not disturbed, dented, damaged, or erased. There is no system of break ups and making up to the other; true love flows Tail Dharavat i.e., uninterrupted, and continuously.

5. Sukshma Taram (very subtle): Lord Ram says in his message to Sita: *Tatva prema kara mama aru tora, janata*

priya eku manu mora. (The reality about the chord of love that binds you and me, dear, is known to my soul alone–II Ram Charita Manas–Sundar Kaand 15.3 II). Love is not a flower, but fragrance. Bapu explained that the word used is Sukshma 'Taram' meaning very subtle, because if it reaches the stage of Sukshma 'Tama' or the subtlest form possible (rather than Taram), it becomes God itself.

6. Anubhav Roopam–True love can only be experienced. It can only be felt and not expressed. Because words have a limit and love is limitless.

Morari Bapu said, the final stage is when you don't have to love but love happens on its own. It is totally self–appearing and effortless. It is no longer an element "to do" but "to be". This stage can only be reached through the grace of God.

Unraveling The Mystique Of Parshuram's Personality

*H*ere's a look at the dynamic yet perplexing character of Bhagavan Parshuram.

In the tradition of 10 avatars in Hinduism, one prominent avatar is Parshuram; Akshaya Tritiya is considered his birth anniversary. In order of appearance, he is sixth in the chain and popularly known as the Avesha Avatar i.e., an incarnation of rage. On Day 32 of Hari Katha, spiritual leader Morari Bapu, explained that an avatar's anger cannot be compared with that of an ordinary human, and it is important not to take it literally, but to understand the meaning of the term through Gurumukh–as explained by a bona fide spiritual master.

"Iron is black, but when it is put in the furnace, it turns red due to excessive heat. Red is not the root colour, as when the iron cools down, it becomes black again," Morari Bapu explained.

In the Ram Charita Manas, Parshuram makes an appearance in the first Canto–Bal Kaand when he arrives enraged at Ram's dispensing Lord Shiva's bow into two to win the hand of Sita.

Tehi avasara suni Siva dhanu bhanga, ayau bhrigukula kamala patanga.1.

(The very moment arrived the sage Parshuram, sun to the lotus-like race of Bhrigu, led by the news of the breaking of the bow.)

II Ram Charita Manas-Bal Kaand 268 II

Describing his physical attributes, Goswami Tulsidas writes:

Gauri sarira bhuti bhala bhraja, bhala bisala tripunda biraja.2.

(A coat of ashes looked most charming on his fair body; his broad forehead was adorned with a 'Tripunda' (a peculiar mark consisting of three horizontal lines, sacred to Lord Shiva)).

II Ram Charita Manas-Bal Kaand 268 II

Parshuram is of fair complexion and has ashes smeared on him. He is a devout follower of Lord Shiva. When we see an axe in his hand, Bapu said it needs to be understood that he used it both to create and destroy. As per the Ram Charita Manas though, an axe represents generosity and donation.

Dana parasu budhi sakti pracanda, bara bigyana kathina kodanda.4.

(Charity is the axe; reason, the fierce lance and the highest wisdom, the relentless bow.)

II Ram Charita Manas-Lanka Kaand 80A II

Parshuram distributes whatever he has gained after waging battles. But because of the tomahawk associated with him, he is automatically considered violent in absence of us obtaining a proper understanding of his real qualities from a bonafide guru, Morai Bapu asserted.

Bapu added that as per his analysis, Parshuram has three outstanding qualities which are mostly associated with the Brahmin community:

1. He is a 'Param Tapasvi': He is a supreme ascetic undertaking severe penance.

2. He is a 'Param Daani': He is a generous donor.

3. He does a lot of Yagna: Prays to the sacrificial fire.

In the Ram Charita Manas, Parshuram demonstrates his anger by saying to Lakshman that his bow is the sacrificial ladle, arrows oblation and his wrath, the blazing fire. He makes mighty princes his victims, whom he cuts into pieces with this very axe and offers as sacrifice. The famous narrator of Ram Katha said that while Parshuram's anger is creative, an ordinary human being's rage is destructive. Parshuram's anger is more of a Leela (performance/pastime) meant to serve a purpose rather than plain rage which is a vice.

The spiritual leader explained that we should not give up these three wonderful attributes of Tapa (penance), Daan (donation) and Yagna as these cleanse and purify our minds again and again.

The moment Parshuram has some time at hand, he goes for penance. He is very liberal in donating. He gave away to Brahmins all the land that he won many times over. He is also the giver of knowledge to the illustrious Karna of Mahabharata.

Concluding, Bapu explained that while penance and Yagnas may not be possible for us, we can interpret them more in line with contemporary times. Our Yagna should not be to make others afraid. We must free people around us from fear and give them encouragement. Chanting of holy name is also the ultimate Yagna. Our penance, especially during any pandemic or crisis, is to follow norms related with our safety and our donation must be in the form of extending cooperation and showing respect to others.

The Incredible Link Between Lord Ganesha And The Alphabet 'V'!

*L*ord Ganesha is one of the most popular deities in the Hindu pantheon. Here's a look at how alphabet "V" defines his various facets.

Ganesha is sketched, illustrated, and worshipped in a multitude of ways. From the twists of a few linear representations around the famous elephant trunk to the elaborate week-long festival in Maharashtra and other parts of the country to celebrate him, Ganesha is the first-worshipped deity in Hinduism. Interestingly, Ganesha Chaturthi also came to be associated with India's struggle for independence from British rule.

Considered extremely astute and wise, Ganesha, the son of Lord Shiva and Goddess Parvati, is known to be a patron of science and the arts. On Day 34 of Hari Katha during Lockdown, spiritual leader Morari Bapu talked about the deity's various facets which are represented through a variety of words and references starting with the alphabet 'V'.

Morari Bapu said that of the several names of Ganesha, one name is Vinayak, which is an amalgam of Vi = Vighnas (difficulties) and Nayak = Leader. So, as Vinayak, he is the leader of Vighnas. This may sound odd and surprising, but that is only the literal meaning. What this actually means is that because he is the leader of difficulties, he has full control over them and does not let problems affect his devotees. He, in fact, is therefore able to remove impediments from our lives, as per Hindu philosophy.

Bapu pointed out that in the introduction of both Ram Charita Manas and Vinay Patrika, the term 'Vinayak' is used in Ganesha Vandana (salutatory prayer). Vinayak also means a special kind of leader; one who is pure and without pretense. He is the one who does not abandon us during our difficult times. The third meaning is that he is filled with 'Vivek' (ability of discernment). And he also has the ability to do 'Vinod' (has a good sense of humour).

Ganesha's stomach is huge, but he is not a hoarder. He is a 'Vairagi' (detached). 'V' also means 'Vichar', i.e., he is a thinker. Vinay Patrika calls him 'Buddhi Vidhata', the giver of thought and intelligence. Morari Bapu explained that, in the same tone, 'V' also means 'Vidvata'-he is extremely learned.

It may be recalled that when Maharishi Veda Vyas incessantly dictated the Mahabharata, it was Ganesha who took up the task to write it all down. The Ram Katha exponent explained that to write anything exactly in the same way as it is uttered requires 'Vidvata', which is in abundance in Ganesha.

Ganesha is also known to be 'Vidya Ke Nayak' (patron of learning)-Adhyatama Vidya (spiritual knowledge), Lok Vidya (folk wisdom), Yoga Vidya (knowledge of yoga) and Veda Vidya (understanding of Vedas). Goswami Tulsidas' Vinay Patrika refers to him as 'Vidya Varidhi', an ocean of learning.

He is known to be 'Vinaysheel' (of polite conduct)–such a person, with or without valid reasons, does not get embroiled in 'Vivad' or conflicts with others.

Ganesha is also the head of all 'Vijay' (victory). He ensures success in all missions and activities if they are well intended. Morari Bapu said that the prayer for accomplishment of tasks should not include the words 'Sarva' Karya Sarvada (all activities always), but rather 'Shubh' Karya Sarvada (activities meant for greater good). The primary object of such work is not to get fruit but further the welfare of the world.

'V' also means 'Vishwa', so he is the leader of the world. Right at the beginning of Vinay Patrika, it is said, 'Gayiye Ganptai Jag Vandan' (we sing the praises of Ganesha who is lauded across the world).

Full Text on Vinay Patrika Verse 1 with meaning:

Gaa'iyē ganapati jagabandana. saṅkara–suvana Bhavānī–nandana. 1.

Sid'dhi–sadana, gaja–badana, vināyaka. kṛpā–sindhu, sundara, saba–lāyaka. 2.

Mōdaka–priya, muda–maṅgala–dātā. vidyā–bāridhi, bud'dhi–vidhātā. 3.

Māṁgata Tulasidāsa kara jōrē. basahiṁ Rāma Siya mānasa mōrē. 4.

Sing the glories of Lord Ganpati (Ganesha), who is revered by the whole world and is the chief of Lord Shiva's followers. He is the beloved son of Lord Shiva and goddess Bhavani (Parvati, the divine consort of Shiva). (1).

He is the abode (treasury; fountainhead) of all Siddhis (mystical powers). His face resembles that of an elephant. He is the eliminator of all obstacles (that come in the way of an individual). He is an ocean of grace, kindness, and benevolence. He is charming and beauteous. And he is able in every respect. (2).

He is very fond of Laddoos (sweetmeat made from gram flour) [Here it means that he is fond of good things, such as wisdom, virtues, auspiciousness, righteousness, probity, propriety, and noble conduct etc.]. He is a bestower of happiness and joys as well as all kinds of auspiciousness and welfare. He is a fathomless ocean of knowledge. And (therefore) he is the Lord of wisdom and intellect. (3).

Goswami Tulsidas requests and pleads, with folded hands and with great earnestness and humility, to such a great Lord (Ganpati, the chief of the attendants of Lord Shiva) that he bless him so that Lord Ram and Sita may reside in his (Tulsidas') heart abidingly for eternity. (4).

Sadhana Panchakam-5 Steps That Can Take You To Nirvana

*A*s advocated by Adi Shankaracharya, here are some easy steps that a devotee can follow to achieve salvation.

Adi Shankaracharya was a powerful, irrepressible spiritual torrent that emerged from Kaladi in Kerala in the 14th century and left an enduring impact on Hindu religious beliefs in the subcontinent. He consolidated the various philosophical currents in Hinduism and established its four main centres so as the conjoin and strengthen its structure. An ardent advocate of Advaita or non-duality, he wrote compelling and definitive commentaries on the Vedas, Upanishads, Brahma Sutras, and the Bhagavad Gita. He travelled relentlessly across the length and breadth of the subcontinent propagating and institutionalizing his thesis. What is exemplary is that he achieved his entire life's mission in merely 32 years.

During Day 35 of Hari Katha, Morari Bapu chose five sutras from Adi Shankaracharya's well-known work Sadhana Panchakam.

In the Sadhana Panchakam, which literally means five methods of spiritual practice, Shankara provides 40 steps so as to reach the stage of Nirvana. These five verses are based on the teachings of Vedanta. Each verse has four lines with two steps, altogether making them 40 steps. Of these, Morari Bapu picked five that devotees can follow easily in their daily lives, especially as Adi Shankaracharya's writing is usually very complex and cannot be easily understood by a layman. The famous Ram Katha exponent promised that these five sutras that he had picked were relevant across sects, creeds and nationalities and require no elaborate study. They only required us to live in some moments of love.

1. **Vedo Nityamadhiyatam** (study the scriptures always): Morari Bapu advocated that, if possible, one should read the Ram Charita Manas and Bhagavad Gita regularly, even if it was limited to one Doha or Shloka, though reading at least one page of the Ramayana and one chapter of the Gita daily was highly recommended. Ram Charita Manas, he felt, was the essence of the Vedas and remover of doubt in a devotee. Else, one could read any holy book of one's choice as long as it was correctly interpreted.

2. **Pratidinam Tatpaduka Sevyatam** (approach the pious who is learned in the scriptures. Worship his sandals daily): Bapu explained that if one were committed to a bona fide master, then once must absorb his personality and words rather than ritualistically worshipping him. One should begin one's day and end it by bowing to his sandals, even if it is through mental remembrance. "Remember his padukas (wooden sandals) and words or sutras given by him. Mull over these thoughts daily even if you are not in his close physical proximity," Bapu said.

3. **Budhajanairvadah Parityajyatam** (do not argue with the learned): We must desist from getting into a controversy

or arguments with a person who is either older than us or more experienced and learned. A person who is wise and full of discretion must be respected. We can remain silent or change the course of conversation if we are at odds with the learned person's thinking. For those who are younger, we must shower them with our love, and for equals, one should extend a hand of friendship.

4. **Pratidinam Bhiksausadham** (cure the disease of hunger. Swallow daily the medicine which is in the form of alms): Adi Shankaracharya has called hunger a disease which must be cured with the medicine of food. While taking alms is valid for a Bhikshu (monk) or Sadhu, for common people we must eat meals with the mentality that these are alms, Morari Bapu said.

5. **Ekante Sukhamasyatam** (seek happiness in solitude): One should learn to live in solitude. Morari Bapu advocated that a devotee should sit alone or be alone for at least some time in the day as a habit. If one doesn't find time during the day, then he should spend some time with himself in the night before sleeping. Morari Bapu cited Pragyachakshu Swami Sharnanand, who felt that solitude was a school and silence was the lesson. While one can do various activities like yoga or reading or chanting while alone, Bapu recommended that for 5 to 10 minutes one should do nothing at all and just be a witness to our surroundings, and also to our thoughts which will appear and disappear like a stream. However, he warned against adverse thoughts, for an idle mind can be a devil's workshop. This time of doing nothing can also be spent meaningfully in shedding tears while remembering God or one's Guru.

Ramanujacharya: A Great Teacher Of Sri Vaishnavism

The exceptional life of Ramanujacharya comprised deep devotion, astute scholarship, and extraordinary compassion.

Ramanujacharya was a famous theologian and philosopher who was born in 1017 CE in the village of Sriperumbudur in Tamil Nadu. He was one of the most famous propagators of Sri Vaishnavism that is dedicated to the worship of Lakshmi and Narayan. His thesis and interpretations of famous sacred texts have borne the test of time, while his form of devotionalism greatly influenced the Bhakti movement.

Talking about Ramanujacharya on Day 37 of Hari Katha, Morari Bapu said India has had a great tradition wherein most avatars hailed from the north of the country, and most 'Acharyas' (spiritual teachers) came from the south; Ramanujacharya, Nimbarkcharya, Shankaracharya, Vallabhacharya and Madhavacharya being cases in point.

Setting context to Ramanujacharya's line of thought, Morari Bapu explained that each and every thing in this world has three reasons behind it: a) Nimit Karan-token to the cause b) Upadan Karan-aid to the cause c) Sadharan Karan-normal cause.

Bapu explained that while Adi Shankaracharya held 'Brahma Satya and Jagat Mithiya' (God is real, world is an Illusion), and that Brahma or God was the cause of all three reasons behind each occurrence mentioned above, there came a time when a completely opposite thought held sway which iterated that God was false and the world was true–'Jagat Satya, Brahma Mithya' (world is real, God is an illusion) and thus, all that was to do here was to eat, drink and make merry.

However, Ramanujacharya held a third view. He felt that Brahma or God is the reason for the two i.e., Nimit Karan and Upadan Karan but Prakruti or Nature also has a role in the Sadharan Karan.

The great Acharya was also a follower of the Vishistadvaita philosophy, which is one of the most popular schools of Vedanta under which it is believed that God alone exists but is characterized by multiplicity, thus non–dualism of the qualified whole.

Morari Bapu informed that Ramanujacharya's sect is called Sri Samprada where Narayan or Vishnu is central to worship along with his consort Lakshmi.

Ramanujacharya, who lived to the ripe age of 120 years, was a brilliant scholar and learned the Vedas at a supple age. Such was his genius that his own teacher Yadava Prakasa became his student. Ramanujacharya travelled across the country and established many temples including the Ranaganathaswamy Temple in Srirangam where his charisma became a talking point in the town of Tiruchirappalli on the banks of River Cauvery.

Spiritual leader Morari Bapu then told an interesting story. Another famous teacher of that time, Yamunacharya, had invited Ramanujacharya, however the teacher is believed to have passed away just before he arrived. Yamunacharya's disciples then anointed Ramanujacharya on their teacher's seat. At that moment Ramanujacharya noticed that though Yamunacharya's body was lying stiff from death, his three fingers were turned. Everyone was perplexed at what such symbolism could mean. His disciples then turned to Ramanujacharya for an explanation.

Ramanujacharya felt these were indicative of some tasks and made three pronouncements. First of all, he declared that he would write a Bhashya (exposition) on Brahmasutra. Immediately, one finger of the body straightened. Secondly, he declared that he would teach everyone Sharnagati (devotional surrender) and spread peace. The second finger straightened. Thirdly, he vowed to write a commentary on the Shrimad Bhagavad Gita, the third finger straightened.

Though Ramanujacharya was married, he left his family life and took Sanyasa (entered the Renunciate Order).

Morari Bapu then related two more anecdotes. As per one story, Ramanujacharya approached a learned teacher for initiation of Mantra. The teacher apparently returned him 18 times before giving an 18-character mantra which he asked him to keep confidential as it was highly potent, and its chanting would lead to welfare of the world. However, it was not to be disclosed to others, who were not qualified. And though it would help the person who obtains it despite him being non-deserving, the giver would have to go to hell. Ramanujacharya immediately went to a balcony and started shouting it out loud. Aghast, Ramanujacharya was asked the reason for such reckless behaviour. The great Acharya from Tiruchirappalli said that if hundreds of people would obtain salvation from the mantra, he would much rather go to hell! Such was his revolutionary thinking.

In a second incident, once the saint was travelling when he met a farmer in the countryside. The farmer came to the Acharya and reverentially bowed to him and asked him to bless his old, tattered Shrimad Bhagavad Gita. The great master asked the farmer whether he knew how to read or had heard commentaries on the Gita. The farmer responded in the negative. The Acharya then asked him as to why he kept it. The farmer responded that he gained a lot of strength from it and that the Gita made him fearless, as he felt he was under its protection. Thus, he said, if you bless the holy book, my faith will be further strengthened. Ramanujacharya had tears in his eyes. He said to the farmer that we all have read the Gita and written commentaries on it, but you have loved it indeed!

Before entering into a state of Nirvana in Srirangam, Ramanujacharya gave a simple discourse. He asked devotees never to disrespect a Sadhu, take refuge in God, chant the holy name and beware of the villains inside like lust, anger, ego, greed, and delusion.

Tales Of Holy Ganges

Ganga is considered the most sacred river in Hinduism and is believed to remove the sins of those who bathe in her or drink her holy water.

The highly revered River Ganges has been flowing since times immemorial, finding a mention in several ancient holy texts. She takes her form as the Ganga at Devprayag, the point of confluence of the Bhagirathi and Alakananda.

On Day 38 of Hari Katha, leading spiritual light Morari Bapu delved on the various tales associated with the origin of the Ganga. It is said that on the day of Ganga Vishaka Saptami, she first entered the dreadlocks of Lord Shiva. A second story says that this is the day when she got released from the dreadlocks of Lord Shiva and reached a place where Sage Janmu was meditating. But her torrent was so forceful that it disturbed him, and he drank her which stopped her onward flow. Eventually legendary King Bhagirath did severe penance for the salvation of his ancestors and Sage Janmu released her. This was the second avatar of the Ganges in the sense that she became more accessible.

On a philosophical note, Bapu drew a comparison with this incident and said anything that is auspicious normally faces obstacles like when one rises from lower realms to make spiritual progress. Or a realized soul comes down from his lofty heights to earth to help ordinary people.

In the Ramayana, Lord Ram also travelled to the banks of River Ganges after salvaging Ahalya and asked Sage Vishwamitra about the antecedent of the river. After hearing the story of her origin, Ram bathed in her flow and offered donations.

Another version is that Sagar's sons were cursed by Kapil Muni and their release from the spell needed the intervention of the holy Ganga. Many generations went by and at last King Bhagirath did penance and managed to secure their salvation after which the Ganges merged into the sea at Gangasagar.

A totally different account relates to a lore where once Lord Shiva, Sage Narad, Sapta Rishi and Lord Vishnu were all seated, and Narad sang a deeply moving classical piece. Lord Shiva also joined in the recital. So mellifluous was the music that God melted, and this liquid form became the Ganges.

As per the Puranas, in one avatar, God came as Vaman and asked Bali for territory contained within three steps. Bali conceded and Vaman measured the entire Tribhuvana–earth, nether and heaven in those three steps. Lord Brahma is said to put that foot in his Kamandal (ewer) which became the Ganges. From the ewer she entered Shiva's dreadlocks and moved forth.

Ramayana's proponent Morari Bapu then gave alternative explanations to what else can be considered pure like the Ganges:

1. One is the river itself as described above and whose flow was released as a torrential stream from Lord Shiva's dreadlocks.

2. Ram Katha is also a type of Ganga-In the Ramayana it is written that Lord Shiva responds to Parvati when she asked about the tale of Lord Ram: *Puchaiyu Raghupati katha prasanga, sakal lok jag pavani Ganga* (You have asked me to repeat the history of the Lord of Raghus, which is potent enough to sanctify all the spheres even as the Ganga purifies the whole world-II Ram Charita Manas-Bal Kaand-112 II)

3. Devotion: Profound devotion for God and the creator is also considered like the Ganges. *Ram Bhakti Jah Sursari Dhara* (Devotion to Ram represents the stream of the holy Ganga, the river of the celestials)-II Ram Charita Manas-Bal Kaand-2 II. There are nine types of devotion described in the Ram Charita Manas. But Bapu's personal view was that 'Ashrey' (surrender at the feet of God/Guru) and 'Ashru' (tears) are the real definition of devotion.

4. Guru: A Buddhapurush (realized soul) is like the pure Ganges, Bapu said. He takes everyone along irrespective of their backgrounds or timing of when devotees have met him. Guru Bani (Guru's speech) is also like the Ganges. Ideally, devotees should remain silent in front of their master and just listen to him. Gurumukh (literally, the mouth of the Guru. Otherwise meant to allude to his perspective.) is like Gomukha-the place of origin of the Ganges. When his tears roll, think it is 'Prakat Ganga'

(Ganga in physical form), Bapu explained. A Guru is the most holy flow.

5. A widow is Ganga Swaroop: Morari Bapu then gave an esoteric meaning. This is not an external appearance but an internal state. A person who understands 'Swaroop' (the real internal form), that person becomes free from Karma. Widowhood is not desirable, but that Swaroop is a different state.

Lord Ram described River Ganges and her auspicious qualities several times in the Ramayana as the remover of all grief. In the Bhagavad Gita, Lord Krishna calls her his Vibhuti (one of His opulence). Even Angad in the courtroom of Ravan says that Ganges should not be mistaken to be just a river; implying she was like a holy goddess.

Morari Bapu urged listeners to keep Ganga Jal (holy water of the Ganges) in their homes as it was auspicious in the same way as having a Tulsi plant in the house. These are like natural remedies just like cow's milk and ghee. Bapu then asked devotees to add just five drops of Ganga water to their drinking water containers, which in turn would make the entire water holy. The Ganges is believed to destroy all ills arising from our natural actions. Bapu also said that that Ganga Jal should be stored in a neat and clean place.

Sita: Goddess Of Primeval Power

*O*ne of the most poignant and moving sagas is the life of Sita, the consort of Lord Ram.

As per Hindu thought, every activity is mostly governed by three modes of Nature. Satvo Guna (mode of goodness), Rajo Guna (mode of passion) or Tamo Guna (mode of darkness). Explaining the meaning of these, spiritual leader Morari Bapu said on Day 39 of Hari Katha that the act of creation is not possible without Rajo Guna, including the birth of a child. He elucidated that a person who is free from Rajo Guna cannot start any new enterprise or project. Maintenance of anything that has been created–animate or inanimate–is not possible without Satvo Guna, and destruction or putting an end to an event or activity requires Tamo Guna.

An exception to this rule occurs when one reaches the stage of becoming 'Guna Atit' (beyond the three modes of Nature). One great example of this stage, as per Morari Bapu, is that of Goddess Sita. The exponent of the Ramayana said that it is believed that all regular work requires exertion and tribulation, but that is not in the case of Sita, who is the remover of all trouble and sorrow.

In the inauguration of Ram Charita Manas, it is written–Bal Kaand, Shloka 5:

Udbhava sthiti samhara karini klesha harinim,

Sarva sreyas karim Sita natoham Rama vallabham.

(I bow to Sita, the beloved consort of Shri Ram, who is responsible for the creation, sustenance, and dissolution (of the universe), removes afflictions and begets all blessings.)

This description clearly indicates that Sita is the consort of the supreme celestial power and indulges in the pursuit of creation, maintenance, and destruction. However, unlike humans, she requires no effort to carry out any activity. She merely needs to resolve, and everything starts taking place on its own merely through her willpower.

Morari Bapu said that in the Ramayana it is also mentioned that Sita is the provider of 'Nirmal Mati' (refined intellect):

Janakasuta jaga janani janaki, atisaya priya karuna nidhana ki,

Take juga pada kamala manavau, jasu kripa niramala mati pavau.

(Janaki, daughter of Janak and mother of the universe and the most beloved consort of Shri Ram, the fountain of mercy, I seek to propitiate the pair of Her lotus feet, so that by Her grace I may be blessed with refined intellect.)

II Ram Charita Manas–Baal Kaand–18.4 II

The spiritual Guru then cited an example of Saint Ramanujacharya as an example of Nirmal Mati:

It is said that when Ramanujacharya became really old, he needed support to move from Srirangam temple in Tiruchirappalli to the Cauvery Ghat (bank of the River Cauvery) for a bath. As he lived nearly a thousand years ago, the caste divide was very much in force in those days. The Acharya used to keep his hand on a Brahmin while going to the river but after he had bathed, he would take the help of a person from the so-called untouchable (Scheduled Caste) community and then would come back and pray. His disciples were perplexed as to why he was doing such a thing. At best he could have taken the aid of a so-called untouchable while going for a bath, and then cleansed himself and returned by walking back with a Brahmin. However, he seemed to be doing exactly the opposite. Unable to understand the conundrum, they approached their teacher and asked him to explain his thought process.

Ramanujacharya responded by saying that he took two baths. "When I go for a bath, the bath is for my body, which believes that it is a Brahmin, learned teacher et al. Afterwards, I keep my hand on a person from the untouchable community with the same feeling that I am taking my second bath. I am now bathing to get rid of my ego and assumed feeling of superiority."

It is for the same reason that Goswami Tulsidas says that he too wants to cleanse his mind with the blessing of Goddess Sita.

Chaitra Shukla Pratiprada Navmi is considered the date of birth of Sita. She is believed to have been discovered by King Janak when he was ploughing a field to please the rain gods.

Despite the celestial qualities explained above, Sita went through complex situations during her Leela (performance/pastimes) on earth. She faced many ordeals-firstly, after marriage, she went to exile for 14 years along with her husband Ram; in the jungle, Ravan's sister Shupanakha created a fracas which eventually resulted in her abduction; she was made a prisoner in Ashoka Vatika, later went through 'Agni Pariksha' (trial by fire), and then when she returned to

Ayodhya after being rescued from Lanka, some critics used bitter words against her. She was then sent into a second exile in a pregnant state.

Sita, who emerged from the womb of Earth, finally ended her journey by withdrawing into Earth again. Morari Bapu ended on a sombre note saying that humans too emerge from the earth and, at the end, will go back into her.

10 Sins As Per Hindu Thought

'Paap' and 'Punya'–misdeeds and good deeds–as concepts have huge centrality in human thought. So, what are the actions that are considered transgressions and should be avoided?

'Paap' and 'Punya'–our sins and acts of goodness are accounted for as we traverse the journey of life. This is a concept which is common to all faiths. Religion has evolved as a system that helps us lead a moral life where we make a concerted effort to avoid the pit holes of wrong thoughts, words, and actions.

Explaining the same, spiritual leader Morari Bapu said on Day 40 of Hari Katha that though we commit a plethora of mistakes, a Self-Realized soul, or a true spiritual master, whom one can call a 'Buddhpurush' can save us from these.

As per the Smritis in Hindu philosophy, there are 10 types of 'Paap' or sins.

There are three bodily sins; these are expressed through our actions:

1. To steal
2. Indulging in violence that is disallowed by scriptures
3. To Rape

Four sins are committed through words:

1. Usage of bitter words
2. Lying/Uttering falsehood

3. Criticising others

4. Talking without reasons, i.e., talking too much

There are three sins that are committed in our thoughts:

1. Thinking about stealing-conspiring to confiscate someone else's property or wealth or wife (latter would also mean adulterous thoughts)

2. To want harm to come to others

3. To be obstinate and argumentative about our point alone

A realized soul slowly helps a disciple escape the trap of these and relieve him of these habits, slowly but steadily.

In the Ramayana, the 'Guru Ruj' (dust of Guru's feet) has a lot of significance. It has been said by Tulsi that 'Guru Ruj' cleanses the eyes i.e., vision and thoughts of a disciple, removing ill will and unkind acts and establishing virtues in the heart of a disciple.

Bandau guru pada paduma paraga, suruchi subasa sarasa anuraga.

amia murimaya churana charu, samana sakala bhava ruja parivaru.1.

Sukriti Sambhu tana bimala bibhuti, manjula mangala moda prasuti.

jana mana manju mukura mala harani, kiye tilaka guna gana basa karani.2

(I greet the dust of the lotus feet of my preceptor, refulgent, fragrant, and flavoured with love. It is a lovely powder of the life-giving herb, which allays the host of all the attendant ills of mundane existence. It adorns the body of a lucky person even as white ashes beautify the person of Lord Shiva and brings forth sweet blessings and joys. It rubs the dirt off the beautiful mirror in the form of the devotee's heart; when applied to the forehead in the shape of a Tilak (a religious mark), it attracts a host of virtues.)

II Ram Charita Manas–Bal Kaand–Ch 01 II

Morari Bapu went on to the extent to say that for the person who has taken refuge in an accomplished master, he needs nothing further than 'Guru Ruj', for normally a disciple does not have the bodily capacity to absorb the full energy of a Guru.

He also advised that the remembrance of a Guru is his best Puja (worship) and acting in accordance with a Guru's wishes and words is his greatest Seva (service).

Seven Sadhanas Counselled By Sage Veda Vyasa

*H*ere are seven practices that can help an aspirant make progress on the spiritual path.

The great sage Veda Vyasa is the author of one of the two great epics of Hinduism, the Mahabharata. He is known to be the traditional compiler of the Vedas and is believed to have written several important puranas. He has also commented on the various 'Sadhanas' or devotional/meditation practices. Speaking about these on Day 41 of the Hari Katha series, the famous exponent of the Ramayana, Morari Bapu, informed that Veda Vyasa had asked for those interested in pursuing the spiritual path to constantly expand these seven practices. Bapu then drew an analogy of each of the seven recommended 'Sadhanas' with a chapter in the Ram Charita Manas of Goswami Tulsidas and provided context and meaning to them.

1. Naam Sadhana (chanting of the holy name): Morari Bapu said that it has been highly recommended to chant the holy name, particularly the one given by a spiritual master. There are no strict rules for this. In the current epoch Kali Yuga, chanting of the holy name is considered the supreme spiritual practice. For evolved saints, the holy name runs automatically inside them, and their rhythm

of breath follows it. Bal Kaand is representative of Naam Sadhana as there are 9 chopais/quadruped lines (Bal Kaand 18–27) describing the significance of the Holy Name.

In the Ram Charita Manas, Goswami Tulsi concludes the stanzas related with the Holy Name by saying:

Bhaya kubhaya anakha alasahu, nama japata mangala disi dasahu

(The Name repeated either with good or bad intentions, in an angry mood or even lethargically, spreads joy in all the ten directions.)

II Ram Charita Manas–Baal Kaand–Ch 28.1 II

2. Roop Sadhana (remembrance of form): To remember the delightful form of God is considered to be Roop Sadhana. Ayodhya Kaand represents this method of devotion. In the Ramayana, there is elaborate description of how beautiful the swarthy Lord Ram is. Even in temples, the deities are beautifully decorated, especially in shrines in Ayodhya, Somnath and Dwarkadheesh. It is said that if a person concentrates constantly on the 'Roop' (outer beauty) of God, he starts understanding his deity's or his own 'Swaroop' (inner light).

3. Leela Sadhana (remembrance of his pastimes): Listening, singing, or enacting of the various pastimes of the avatars like Ram and Krishna is a form of a spiritual practice. This is represented by the Aranya Kaand where Lord Ram tells Sita that she must now dwell in the fire for some time as he must perform Leela (performance/pastimes), indicating an ensuing war to eliminate Ravan.

Sunahu priya brata ruchira susila, mai kacha karabi lalita naralila.

(Listen, my dear, one who has been staunch in the holy vow of fidelity to me and is so virtuous in conduct: I am going to act a beautiful human pastime.)

II Ram Charita Manas-Aranya Kaand-Ch 24.1 II

4. Dhyaan Sadhana (meditation): This practice is represented by Kishkindha Kaand where a journey must be made inwards. When Hanuman and the monkeys enter Swayamprabha's cave in search of food and water, she advises them to close their eyes and wait, for they would be transferred to where Sita is in Ashoka Vatika. This was indicative of an internal journey that would help them make progress in their mission. However, the monkeys opened their eyes in between and found themselves by the sea. There are also other references in the Ramayana like, 'Sankar sahaj swaroop sambhala' (Bal Kaand Ch 58.4), meaning Lord Shiva connected with his inner self. Hanuman too collects his thoughts just before embarking on his mission to Lanka.

5. Smaran Sadhana (practice of remembrance): After Sita is abducted by Ravan and is sitting in the Ashok Vatika, she is described to be constantly remembering Lord Ram.

Krisa tanu sisa jata eka beni, japati hridaya Raghupati guna sreni.

(Emaciated in body, she wore a single braid of matted hair on Her head and repeated to Herself the list of Lord Rama's excellences)

II Ram Charita Manas–Sundar Kaand–Ch 4 II

In the same chapter, Hanuman says–

Kaha Hanumanta bipati prabhu soi, jaba tava sumirana bhajana na hoi.

(Said Hanuman: There is no misfortune other than ceasing to remember and adore You.)

II Ram Charita Manas– Sundar Kaand–Ch 32.2 II

6. Dham sadhana (fondness for the places associated with a deity): This is clearly the Lanka Kaand where Lord Ram not only eliminated all the demons in the battle in Lanka, but also granted them a place in his home as Nirvana. And as Ravan is put to death, his widow Mandodari eulogizes Lord Ram:

Ajanma te paradroha rata papaughamaya tava tanu ayam

Tumhahu diyo nija dhama rama namami brahma niramayam

(This body of yours had taken delight from its very birth in harming others and was a sink of multitudinous sins; yet Lord Rama has absorbed you in His own being! I bow to Him, the immutable Brahma)

II Ram Charita Manas–Lanka Kaand–Chhand 104 II

7. Purna or Shunya Sadhana (emptiness or completeness): It is a known factor in spirituality that one needs to either obtain completeness or emptiness. Either way we achieve absolute peace. Bapu explained that what is extraordinary

is that the person who has perfected himself is also either completely empty or totally full, like Bhusundi or the Guru in Mahakal temple in Uttar Kaand.

Morari Bapu added that we should examine our own body as a holy book. We will find that all these seven chapters are inside us and that we too can undertake all these practices and return to our immaculate form and find peace.

Dispositions And Categories Of A Guru

A Guru has been a subject of enigma since the time a Master–Disciple relationship started. Here is a closer look at the entity of a Guru.

Guru is a spiritual light who guides and leads a disciple. But there is much mystique surrounding him and one is curious about how to identify a guru and discern his traits. During Day 42 of the Hari Katha series, a viewer posed a question to spiritual leader Morari Bapu about the various types of Vrutti (dispositions) and Varg (categories) of Gurus.

Morari Bapu began by stating that a true Guru is one who keeps the disposition of inaction or detachment while undertaking all activities, and even when he is inactive, he is engrossed in action but without expectation of any fruit. It is impossible to state the true glory of a Sadaguru, he stated.

Bapu said a Guru imparts two great gifts to a disciple. Firstly, he does 'Shruti Daan', which means he imparts knowledge including that of the scriptures. Secondly, he gives 'Smruti Daan', which is allegorical of Bhakti (devotion) through constant remembrance of God and Guru.

Morari Bapu explained that a Guru is imbued with 6 prominent Vruttis or types of dispositions as per the Ram Charita Manas of Goswami Tulsidas:

1. Ganesha Vrutti: A person whose Mun (mind), Buddhi (intellect) and Chit (psyche) are not fickle, or rather these are balanced. Representative of Ganesha, an elephant shows greater equilibrium and advancement compared to other animals on these three fronts. A Guru is also egoless.

2. Gauri Vrutti: Lord Shiva's consort is representative of Shraddha or devotion. A Guru has deep devotion within himself and is a subject of devotion for his disciple. The famous exponent of Ramayana explained that sometimes a disciple displays negative traits like anger, criticism or even insults, but when he realizes his mistake and comes back with tears, a Guru accepts him; such is a Guru's devotion for his student.

3. Ganga Vrutti: The Ganges has a long circuitous route; she emanates in the heavens as she travels from Brahma to Vishnu to Mahesh and then touches earth at Gangotri and later Devprayag, travels to Rishikesh, Haridwar, Prayag and finally submerges into the ocean at Gangasagar. The Guru also leaves his abode and travels great distances to reach his disciples, remains ever flowing, fresh and new.

4. Gau Vrutti: Like a cow, a Guru is simple and free from crookedness. He remains equipoised in loss or gain. There is a certain Sahajta (naturalness) in all that he does.

5. Gagan Vrutti: In him, the trait of sky's vastness exists. Whether it is his largesse or the fact that he cannot be measured, he is like the firmament.

6. Gun Grahak Vrutti-A guru collects what is good and auspicious from everywhere. Like a bird sucking honey from various flowers, a Guru absorbs the best from wherever he gets it.

There are also six categories of Gurus:

1. Param Guru: He is the ultimate or supreme guru. Like Lord Shiva, he is Tribhuvani guru or reigns in all three spheres of existence–heaven, earth and nether. No one is above him and all cosmic activity occurs through his grace. He is not visible, but we can feel his grace in an invisible form all around us.

2. Sadaguru: He is in physical form and lives amongst us. He is one whom everyone loves; not just humans, but also stars, comets, planets, birds, plants, trees, and all of Nature. Even if one doesn't want, one is attracted towards him. One can behold him in various types of relationships, but everyone wants to be associated with him. Whether through Prem (love) or Vair (animosity), no one can ignore him.

3. Jagat Guru: Is the Guru of the whole world. In Krishna's salutation we say, 'Krishnam Vande Jagadgurum'. Such a Guru is lauded and celebrated in the whole world.

4. Dharam Guru: He mostly represents a religion or sect and is even feared by people for he talks of sin, punishment, and atonement; he sometimes might even get angry.

5. Kul Guru: He is the one who is mostly associated with a family or a community. But when he sometimes enforces certain rigid notions forcefully, there is even a chance of some disciples rebelling. In the Ramayana, Samudra is described as Lord Ram's Kul Guru but when the sea refused to give him passage to Lanka, Ram picks up his bow and arrow.

6. Kapati Guru: These are not real gurus but pretenders and defraud disciples and mislead them.

Spiritual light Morari Bapu advised that it is best not to attempt to understand a Guru. If one has taken refuge of a true Guru, then it is sufficient that the Guru has understood that person and has accepted him and given him shelter.

The Legend And Life Of Prahlad And Narasimha Avatar

*T*he story of Prahlad is one of supreme devotion.

Among the pantheon of supreme devotees of God, one name sparkles and that is of Prahlad. Born into a demon's family, he had all the saintly attributes that are extensively described in the Puranas. A treatise in the Srimad Bhagavatam is attributed to Prahlad in which he describes the process of loving worship of God. Speaking on Day 43 of the Hara Katha series, spiritual leader Morari Bapu picked the subject of Prahlad and the various challenges that he faced. Bapu quoted the Ram Charita Manas in which Prahlad is referred to as 'Bhakta Siromani' (supreme devotee).

"Naamu Japat Prabhu Kinhaa Prasadu, Bhagata Siromani Bhaye Prahladu."

(It was because of his repeating the Holy Name that the Lord showered His grace on Prahlad, who thereby became the crest-jewel amongst devotees)

II Ram Charita Manas-Bal Kaand-Ch 26.2 II

Bapu, who is a great proponent of the Ramayana, explained that there are two or three main protagonists who are referred to as 'Bhakta Siromani' in the epic. Other than Prahlad, Lord

Ram's younger brother Bharat and Lord Vishnu's vehicle Garuda are considered great devotees.

Commenting on the life of Prahlad, Bapu said that though his childhood was "Kashtamayi" (full of perils), his entire life was "Ishtamayi" (devoted to God). As a young boy, one after another, troubles chased Prahlad, the youngest of the four sons of the fiend Hiranyakashipu.

Bapu narrated that Hiranyasksha and Hiranyakashipu were two brothers of whom the former was slayed by God in the form of Varaha avatar. From the time of Hiranyasksha's death, Hiranyakashipu thirsted for revenge and became a sworn enemy of Vishnu. He also felt that demigods were the real culprits who misguided Vishnu into indulging in acts that served their purpose. Hiranyakashipu thus ordered all demons under his command to kill demigods and himself went to do penance on Mount Mandranchala to gain the boon of immortality. At that time, his wife Kayadhu was pregnant with Prahlad.

Hiranyakashipu's austerities were severe as he stood for years on his foot thumb until he finally received a blessing from Brahma that no living entity created by him could kill him. He also asked as a boon that he should not die inside or outside any residence, during daytime or at night, nor on the ground or in the sky, not by any weapon, nor by any human being or an animal. Having put multiple and such formidable conditions, Hiranyakashipu attacked all the worlds in heaven and on earth and established his supremacy.

Bapu continued with the narration saying that one day while Prahlad was studying under Shukracharya, the teacher taught him the principles of Dharma, Artha and Kama, but the young boy intervened to say that these are applicable for people engrossed in duality and that one should rather take refuge of God. When Hiranyakashipu was petting his son in his lap and asked him about what his teacher taught him at school, Prahlad repeated the conversation and spoke about the various modes of Bhakti (devotion). This enraged his father to no end as he opposed Vishnu vehemently, so much so that after failing to transform his son's thinking through persuasion or reprisal, he then used force and attempted to kill him again and again, failing each time. Prahlad was thrown off a mountain; attempts were made for an elephant to trample him and to kill him in a raging fire. The young boy was saved each time.

Finally, Hiranyakashipu challenged his son asking that God should also be in his palace's pillar if he is supposed to be everywhere, to which the latter responded in the affirmative. Because Prahlad had been so severely tested but never lost his devotion, God appeared in the form of Narasimha from the pillar and slaughtered Hiranyakashipu tearing his chest with his nails on the threshold of his palace. Narasimha fulfilled all the conditions of the boon-he was an avatar thus not created by Brahma, he was half human and half animal; he killed the demon king in his lap, thus neither on ground or sky; on the threshold, thus not inside or outside; at dusk, therefore it was neither day or night; and with his nails, thus not using any weapons.

It is said that Narasimha was in such rage at that time that even the demigods feared to go close to him and eulogize or thank him for eliminating Hiranyakashipu. Finally, Prahlad was sent forward and was instantly taken into his lap by Narasimha and lovingly licked.

Spiritual leader Morari Bapu revealed that later too Prahlad showed supreme qualities of honesty and humility, winning over his senses and serving the Brahmins. When God asked him for a Kamna (boon), he said desires should not arise in him at all, such was his wisdom.

After concluding the tale of his life, Morari Bapu said a supreme devotee is one who has gone beyond Mun (mind), Buddhi (intellect), Chit (psyche) and Ahankar (ego), and indeed Prahlad had transcended all these.

The Inspiring Life Of Gautam Buddha

*B*uddha Purnima is the day on which Gautam Buddha was born, and also achieved Nirvana, leaving behind his fundamental message of compassion.

Buddha Purnima is a unique day as Siddhartha Gautam was both born and achieved Nirvana on the same day over 2500 years ago. On Day 44 of Hari Katha, spiritual leader Morari Bapu spoke on the subject of Buddha. Describing his life, Bapu said that just seven days after he was born under a tree in Lumbini, his mother passed away. Siddhartha was raised by his mother's sister Gautami, who was his father Shudhodhan's second wife. He was called Gautam after his foster mother, and also because he was born into the Gautam Gotra (name of paternal lineage). Otherwise, his name was Siddhartha, meaning one who is born with Siddhis (paranormal or mystical powers).

Bapu said Siddhartha came to be known as Buddha because he achieved Buddhatva, or the highest wisdom. He was also called Tathagata and imparted many morals through his life.

Siddhartha was born into a royal family and was married to the utterly beautiful Yashodhara, with whom he had a son Rahul. It is said that Siddhartha was a very charismatic personality, who was not only highly skilled but extensively trained in administration and politics. He was an ace in horse racing but during competitions his compassion compelled him to let his closest rival win just near the finishing line. Morari Bapu added a line here that on the path of spirituality, losing has a huge significance, saying, "Jeetey so Sikander, hare wo Kalandar (one who wins is an emperor, one who loses is a mystic).

The scale of opulence surrounding the life of Siddhartha was unlimited. He had three palaces, one for each season. His palace for summers remained cool, one for winters stayed warm, and there was another for the rainy season. When he was very young, an ascetic had predicted that either he would become a magnificent king or a highly elevated sage. Fearing that Gautam might pursue the spiritual path, his father Shudhodhan deliberately kept him away from all sorrow, so much so that till his youth Siddhartha did not even know that misery existed.

But fate had other plans. One day during an outing, Siddhartha saw a frail old man. Shocked to see how advanced years had ravaged his body, Siddhartha asked his charioteer whether age afflicts all humans. An affirmative response made an intense impact on his psyche as he felt a deep wound inside; the first petal opened.

A few days later he saw a man in pain, suffering from disease. Siddhartha asked his charioteer whether ailments can cripple anybody. An affirmative answer opened the second petal, said Morari Bapu.

Next, Gautam saw a procession where men were carrying a dead body. On questioning him about why the man was lifeless, his charioteer informed him that all those who are born must die one day. The third petal opened inside him.

Siddhartha Gautam left home and undertook such severe penance and austerities that his body was reduced to a skeletal state, and he had no energy left. It was then that he heard a group of village belles singing that the strings of an instrument should neither be too tight or too loose because then they would not be able to produce music. A chord immediately struck with Siddhartha, as he felt that neither should a person wallow too much in luxury nor should he torture his body. The answer lay in the middle path.

Incessantly meditating and resisting all temptations, Siddhartha achieved enlightenment under a tree in Gaya. Morari Bapu explained that each individual has a right to Buddhahood, but we should not become Udaas (depressed) rather be Udaseen (detached). The spiritual leader emphasized that the sacrifices that Buddha made were unparallel and he had declared that he would not accept Nirvana for himself till the last person on earth had been freed from bondage of misery.

Buddha gave lessons to a few disciples who took the lamp around the world espousing his four noble truths:

1. There is sorrow or suffering in this world.
2. There is cause or origin of sorrow
3. It is possible to end sorrow
4. The path that leads to a cessation of sorrow also leads us to Samadhi

He then gave the 8-fold path to bring all grief and misery to an end:

1. Right View
2. Right Resolve or Intention
3. Right Speech
4. Right Conduct or Action
5. Right Livelihood
6. Right Effort
7. Right Mindfulness
8. Right Samadhi to achieve equanimity

Spiritual leader Morari Bapu continued by saying that Buddha advised against robbery, criticism, gluttony, gambling and hurting others. He felt there should be Sahajta or naturalness in speech, action, and appearance.

Despite all these teachings, the core essence of Buddha's life and messages remains compassion. Morari Bapu said Buddha is compassion incarnate. His eyes, feet, hands, touch, words, and vision are all defined by compassion. Later, his family members like his foster mother Gautami, his cousin Ananda, wife Yashodhara, and son Rahul, all got initiated and achieved the highest wisdom.

One day, the food that Buddha ate as alms was stale, and poisoned him, becoming the cause for his death. Falling severely ill after consuming that meal, Buddha called his disciples and told them that he had only little time left in this world but warned anyone against harming the family that had served him contaminated dinner. Buddha said that he had only gratitude for the man who served him food. "My mother gave me birth and this man has given me death," he said.

Among Buddha's attendants and disciples who grieved the most was Ananda, who said he didn't want anything in life, not even Nirvana. He only wanted Buddha. Buddha gave his Padukas (wooden sandals) which were filled with his consciousness as a blessing to him.

Buddha was born, passed away and achieved enlightenment, all on a full moon day. Though he was highly educated and erudite, he spread his message in the Pali language that was simple to understand for the common man.

Morari Bapu continued with an interesting interpretation to Buddha and his teachings. Firstly, Bapu said Samadhi should be seen as a state in which a person has been freed from "Aadhi (old age), Vyadhi (disease) and Upadhi (death)." Obviously, each person must face these, but what this means is that one should be able to go through these stages without any fear. The Samadhi that Buddha achieved was perennial. Secondly, Bapu explained that lack of wisdom is the cause of anger, and the lack of love causes malice and hatred towards others.

In today's day and age, Morari Bapu said, 'Buddham Sharanam Gacchami can be interpreted as "Shudham Sharanam Gacchami"–one must take the refuge of the pure. "Sangham Sharanam Gacchami can be construed as "Sangam Sharanam Gacchami" meaning that we must enable societal alliances, dialogue, and reconciliation. "Dhamma Sharanam Gacchami" should be seen as "Dhanyam Sharanam Gacchami" meaning that we must leave everything to the supreme one.

Silence And Sadhus-The Importance Of Maun

There are different stages of 'Maun' or vows of silence. What is that a disciple experiences?

Have you heard the sound of silence? Keeping 'Maun', or maintaining a vow of silence, is an important practice on this path. Speaking on Day 46 of Hari Katha about 'Maun', Morari Bapu said that Astitva (the universe) and Buddhpurush (a realized soul) listen to our words and silences even if no one else does. Morari Bapu is a strong advocate of maintaining 'Maun', as this was recommended by his Sadaguru, Tribhuvana Das Dada, as one of the 5 essential practices.

Bapu said that just because we don't know how to listen to silence or unsaid thoughts, it does not mean that the universe is not listening. Just like an illiterate man is awestruck by someone reading a newspaper; the former wonders about how the other person would be deciphering words.

Delving deeper into the subject, Morari Bapu explained that a Sadhak or a practitioner of 'Maun' passes through three phases:

1. In the first stage one starts hearing external noise in a more pronounced way. We become more attentive and aware of the sounds all around us like the birds, Nature,

or general domestic or workplace activities that are in motion.

2. In the second stage or medium stage of 'Maun', whatever may be the level of noise outside, one hears nothing at all. The disciple's awareness turns inwards, and he starts hearing internal sounds. It is the noise within us that has been suppressed for many births due to various reasons.

3. The last or final stage of Maun is when a Sadhak enters 'Anant Maun' or the zone of limitless silence. One becomes oblivious to both external and internal sounds. This period is very auspicious but also extremely frightening because we are drawn towards absolute silence. Our body and mind don't have the capacity to withstand such extreme, unending, and complete silence. This stage can be very disturbing and delicate, and a disciple can turn insane. The devotee needs the guidance and help of a true guru at this point. Constant remembrance of God also helps him in reaping rich dividends of the experience.

Before concluding his extremely insightful discourse, Morari Bapu shared his thoughts on three types of Sadhus or Sages that occurred to him that morning:

1. 'Mun Ka Sadhu'–Sage of the Mind: In the Ramayana, Lord Ram can be described as 'Mun Ka Sadhu' as he was able to maintain equanimity despite the highs and lows of life and accepted changing conditions.

2. 'Vachan Ka Sadhu'–Sage of Speech: Lord Shiva can be called a 'Vachan Ka Sadhu' as from his mouth emerged words that dispelled the darkness of Parvati's ignorance

and we received the gift of the Ramayana which has purified all the three worlds (earth, heaven, nether).

3. 'Karam Ka Sadhu'–Sage of Action: Indeed, Hanuman fits the bill as 'Karam Ka Sadhu' as he is the prime devotee of Lord Ram and accomplished several tasks for him with skill, competence, and success.

While different people can have different traits of Sadhus, there is one common characteristic that marks all Sadhus and that is that he is egoless and has no conflict with anyone in the world and is thus protected by Astitva.

The 10 Faces Of Ravan

*T*here is a special meaning attached to the 10 faces of Ravan, the demon king of Lanka and one of the main protagonists of the *Ramayana.*

Ravan is a dreaded demon, the main villain of the Ramayana, and central to its theme. It is a well-known tale that when Lord Ram and Sita were in exile, Ravan abducted Sita and took her to Lanka. Lord Ram and his monkey army finally defeated and killed Ravan and freed Sita, before returning to Ayodhya, from where they had been banished for 14 years. What is interesting about Ravan is his multi-faceted personality. Though he is a demon who has terrorized gods and goddesses, he has done much penance, is a devotee of Lord Shiva and a master of the Vedas.

Intriguingly, he has 10 heads or faces because of which he is also called 'Dus Mukh'. Speaking on Day 48 of Hari Katha, Morari Bapu recalled how his Sadaguru, Tribhuvana Das ji, explained to him what each of Ravan's 10 faces represented.

Just like darkness precedes light, the avatar of Ravan is mentioned before the appearance of Lord Ram in the Ram Charita Manas written by Goswami Tulsidas. Ramayana is thus, in a sense, a journey from darkness to light. Bapu recollected how the moral of his primary school prayer was in similar vein:

*"Asatyo Mahi Thi Prabhu Param Satya Tu Laye Ja. Unda
Andhaare Thi Prabhu Param Teje Tu Laye Jaa."*

(Oh Lord! Take me from falsehood to ultimate truth, take
me from deep darkness to supreme light.)

Morari Bapu explained that 'Mukh' (mouth) as in the name
of Dusmukh (Ravan) is representative of Bhog (enjoyment of
pleasure) while 'Rath' (chariot) as in the name of Dasratha is
representative of Saiyyam (constraint). Both don't go hand in
hand; a person has to choose one and give up the other.

It is about these 10 faces of Ravan that the spiritual guide
elaborated:

1. Ninda Mukh: Ravan used to criticize others. Bapu said
   that he would personally never ask anyone to give up
   'Nidra (sleep) but urged listeners to totally give up 'Ninda'
   (criticizing others).

   In the Ram Charita Manas, it is written:

   'Par ninda sam agha na garisa'

   (There is no sin an equal to being critical of others)

   II Ram Charita Manas, Uttar Kaand-121. A-11 II

2. Mukharta: Ravan was extremely vocal. He spoke
   endlessly. Any person who speaks in excess becomes less
   committed to dialogue and more involved in dispute.
   Speaking too much is like a disease.

3. Jalpana or Vitandavaad Mukh: These are archetypal
   words which mean to utter nonsense. Many a times,
   Ravan spoke ill thought-out or fanatical words.

4. Aham Garjan Mukh: Ravan's were egoistic declarations.

5. Pralap Mukh: Bapu explained that this is a typical state when there is so much anger in us that our eyes are filled with rage, causing tears.

6. Asatya Mukh: Ravan spoke lies several times.

7. Durmukh: When one is filled with the feeling of revenge, the distorted expression on the face is Durmukh.

8. Grass Mukh: A Bhogi (enjoyer of pleasure) wants to consume everything.

9. Bhim Mukh: This represents fierceness or ferocity.

10. Veda Mukh: This is Ravan's only sweet and positive face. His tongue utters Vedas and their meanings.

Morari Bapu has done 10 Ram Kathas on the subject of Ravan.

The 10 Chariots Of Dasratha Of Ayodhya

There are esoteric meanings behind the word Dasratha which outline the major characteristics of Lord Ram's father.

In continuing with the series related with 'Dus Mukh' of Ravan (Chapter 42), on Day 49 of Hari Katha, spiritual guide Morari Bapu, took forth the conversation talking about the Dus Rath (10 chariots) of Dasratha, the King of Ayodhya and the father of Lord Ram. Dasratha has been described as King Manu in his previous birth wherein he had done a lot of penance along with his wife Shatrupa, after which he received a boon that God himself would be born as a son to him in his next birth. Manu and Shatrupa then appear as Dasratha and Kaushalya in Ayodhya, and Lord Ram is born to them. As explained to Morari Bapu by his Sadaguru, Tribhuvana Das ji, Dasratha is one whose chariot moves in all 10 Dishas (directions).

Morari Bapu then explained the 10 chariots of Dasratha:

1. Manorath: This is a type of wish wherein one desires something but leaves the fulfilment in the hands of God. In his birth as Manu, Dasratha desired a son like God, a wish that was fulfilled. He also wanted intense love for his progeny so much so that his own life would depend upon

him. Separation would spell death, which is what happened when Lord Ram went to exile. Dasratha also wished to see Ram installed on the throne of Ayodhya, but this was a desire that remained unfulfilled. The lesson here is that though we are free to desire, we should remain satisfied irrespective of whether our wish is realized or not. Bapu said if our desire is accomplished, we should see it as God's grace and if it is not, then as God's will.

2. Dharma Rath: There is an elaborate description of Dharma Rath in the Ram Charita Manas, which Lord Ram encapsulates to Vibhishan in the middle of battlefield when the latter was grief stricken to see Ram without chariot and sandals. Many of the characteristics of the chariot of Dharma include courage, patience, truth, discretion, and faith in Guru. All these traits are found in Dasratha.

3. Dev Rath: This term is used particularly in context with Indra Rath, the one that Indra had sent for Lord Ram along with charioteer Matali. After his demise, Dasratha went to Dev Lok but returned to meet Lord Ram after the battle with Ravan was over. The vehicle he used was Dev Ratha.

4. Jeevan Rath: Bapu quoted lines from Atharva Veda:

   Anuvratah Pituh Putro Maatraa Bhavatu Samanah

   Jaayaa Patye Madhu Mateem Vaacham Vadatu Shaantivam

   (Let son be loyal to father, and of one mind with his mother. Let a wife speak to her husband words, that are honey-sweet and gentle.)

This advice is quintessentially the crux of life, wherein a child (who represents love) is loyal to the father (who represents truth) and follows the instructions of a mother (who represents compassion). Later in life, he aspires for a wife with whom he has a loving relationship. Dasratha's wives are described as ideal.

Kausalyadi nari priya saba acarana punita, pati anukula prema drida hari pada kamala binita.

(Kausalya and his other beloved consorts were all of holy life; humble and devoted to their lord, they had a strong attachment to the lotus feet of Sri Hari.)

II Ram Charita Manas-Bal Kaand-Do:188 II

5. Ram Rath: This means a life that is filled with Ram or God. Dasratha had the name of Ram on his lips, and it is his name that he uttered six times when death came to him.

6. Kama Rath: Dasratha is not just a Ram Rathi but a charioteer of Kama (lust) as well. He was totally besotted by his wife Kaikeyi. Though he is a king of great valour, he is frightened when he hears that his dear Kaikeyi is upset with him.

7. Bhagirath: Bhagirath brought the Ganges on earth to give nirvana to his ancestors. Bhagirath symbolises a do or die attitude, which is also seen in Dasratha.

8. Swarg Rath: This is the chariot that Dasratha would use when he travelled from earth to visit his friend Indra in heaven.

9. Deh Rath: Dasratha's body is also a chariot. It is a vehicle wherein the two legs confer movement. Hands are the reins which help maintain equanimity of Karma. The vision of a person is the charioteer. A person should have courage and discretion in movement.

10. Abhi Rath: This comes from the word 'Abhi' which means now–that particular moment. One should always live in the present. It is also a 'Snakalpa ka Rath', meaning whatever one thinks happens immediately. Dharma also sometimes feels disheartened. Dasratha, who is known to be 'Dharama Dhuranadhar', feels deep sorrow that he has not been blessed with a child. Immediately, he acts and goes to his Guru to find a solution.

Abandon Useless Thoughts, Do Not Repeat Mistakes

What should be the guiding principles of our life? Self–introspection could be the key to improvement among others.

Swami Sharnanand, who founded the Manav Seva Sangh, lost his eyesight at the tender age of 10, which he felt was the cause of his misery. However, on listening to several religious persons who visited his home when he was child, he realised that most people were unhappy. And the root cause of their unhappiness was desire. He tried with determination to create a mentality of staying equanimous and embarking on the path of self-enquiry and truth.

On Day 50 of the Hari Katha series, spiritual leader Morari Bapu delineated the basic principles of 'Manavta', or humanity as espoused by Swami Sharnanand. Bapu validated that these were golden words and could be very useful if followed.

The 11 principles are as follows:

1. To do self-introspection by using prudence and observing one's own faults and not that of others.

2. After realizing one's own mistakes, we should try and not repeat those errors by having strong determination and firm faith in God.

3. To use the concept of justice on oneself but that of forgiveness for others.

4. Self-improvement by:

   a) Controlling sense organs, meaning balanced enjoyment of senses

   b) By serving others

   c) Remembrance of God

   d) Embarking on journey of discovery of truth.

5. Not to treat others duty as one's own right, mistake others kindness as outcome of our superior qualities, and others weakness as one's own strength.

6. Having affection towards all human beings despite not having any sort of relations with them whatsoever. This is similar to the thought of 'Vasudeva Kutumbakam' (the whole world is a family).

7. To serve others as per one's own strength and capability.

8. To observe restraint in diet and self-dependency in daily chores.

9. To become loveable and useful to all by the way of doing good work with body, controlling one's mind, right use of intellect, love in the heart and erasing ego.

10. To give importance to objects over money, persons over objects, prudence over persons, and truth over prudence.

11. To brighten one's future by abandoning useless thoughts and making right use of the present.

In the next day of the discourse i.e., on Day 51 of Hari Katha, Bapu was asked about steps that one should take, if a person has committed a mistake, Bapu said that rather than going into tedious rituals to cleanse oneself, a person should openly admit one's mistake to the person who has been wronged as per the concept of 'Atma Nivedanam'.

How A Guru Shapes A Disciple Like A Clay Pot

What are the stages that a disciple goes through as he is prepared for perfection–here are the answers as per Kabir.

Enough can never be written about a Guru and disciple relationship in the spiritual realm. Speaking on Day 51 and Day 52 as part of the Hari Katha series, Morari Bapu talked about this vital relationship. He explained that a Sadhu plays several roles for the disciple, like that of a farmer, wherein he protects the sapling but removes the weeds; a sevak-a guru actually serves the disciple; a doctor, protector; and a 'Khojak or Shodhak', which means a discoverer of science and spirituality.

Morari Bapu then drew an analogy of a potter and a clay pot and that of a Guru and a disciple, while responding to a query from a listener. The spiritual leader quoted saint Kabir on the subject and explained that a Guru helps the one who has taken his refuge to travel through all five chief elements to do Navnirman (recreate) of his personality.

Clay, that is derived from earth, makes us tolerant and patient, water brings together the smallest of atoms, the sky enlightens us about Ghatakash (space within us) as well about

Mahaakash (universe), the air purifies through touch and fire ensures that a protégé goes through trial by fire.

In the role of a potter, when a Guru moulds clay (in this context a disciple) by striking it and tapping it, a disciple might feel that a Guru is being harsh, but in fact he is giving shape to his personality through his personal attempts. Bapu pointed out that one should not forget that a Guru always keeps one hand inside the pot, which means unseeingly he always has the back of his disciple, giving him loving support.

When the pot is ready, a Guru puts the pot in the market, which means that he then sees the interaction of his devotee with the world. Through myriad experiences, the pot is tested as customers tap to see its sturdiness. Keeping the pot in the market also means that a ripened devotee is readied to serve society after passing through all stages of learning.

An example Morari Bapu cited was of the monks that Gautam Buddha prepared and sent across the world to travel and spread the message of the Sangha. The disciple is readied for the welfare of society–'Sarva Bhoot Hitai'.

This is a very unique and interesting experience, and it is said that all elements of Nature keep an eye on the devotee and the process. They observe our development. Each disciple should have the awareness that someone is watching even when he or she is alone. The sun, moon, stars, air, fire, water, Disha (directions), earth, our own conscience, Yamraj (God of death), day and night, and dharma are constantly observing our activities.

How To Establish The Auspicious And Remove The Inauspicious From Your Life

*G*oswami Tulsidas' verse shows how a Sadhu or a spiritual master brings joy, beauty, and good tidings to our lives.

During Day 53 of the Hari Katha series, spiritual leader Morari Bapu elaborated on an interesting piece of writing in the Dohavali Ramayana of Goswami Tulsidas. Giving a personal touch to the discourse, Bapu recollected how there was a green cupboard with several compartments, in his childhood home, where his grandfather and guru Tribhuvana Das ji kept many sacred texts including the old version of the Dohavali Ramayana. The new version of Gita Press has slight changes.

According to the Dohavali Ramayana, there are seven things that Goswami ji feels will help establish Mangal (auspicious) by removing Amangal (inauspicious).

As per the new version of Gita Press, Tulsi Das writes:

Sudha Sadhu Surtaru Suman Suphal Sumanagal Baat

Tulsi Sita Pati Bhakti Sab Sumangal Sath

In the older version of Dohavali Ramayana the verse remains the same, but the word Sadhu comes before Sudha and starts the couplet....*Sadhu Sudha Surtaru*...

As per Morari Bapu, each of the words of the verse represent a canto of the Ram Charita Manas. The word Sadhu is indicative of 'Bal Kaand', Sudha of 'Ayodhya Kaand', Surtaru of 'Aranya Kaand', Suman of 'Kishkindha Kaand', Suphal of 'Sundar Kaand', Sumangal Baat of 'Lanka Kaand' and Ram Bhakti of 'Uttar Kaand'.

Goswami Tulsidas says a Sadhu always establishes what is propitious in our lives; it is only that we must identify the right person as being a spiritual master and then have full faith in him.

A Sadhu denotes a spiritual master who is like a gardener. God owns the garden, but it is a Sadhu who tends it in a way that all its flowers fully blossom and spread fragrance, and trees give fruit which are beneficial to others. In terms of people, a master brings positivity in the body, the mind, and our fortune.

A true spiritual master is either fully empty from inside or totally complete as per the principle of 'Shunya' or 'Purna'. Morari Bapu thus said, "A Sadhu is a Mali (gardener) and Andar Se Khali (experiencing emptiness from inside) and Hum Sab Ka Wali (our protector)." Just like a guardian takes responsibility of a child and his report card at school, similarly a Sadhu takes responsibility of all our deeds and actions despite our shortcomings and vices like greed, envy, and hatred.

It is only apposite for us to extend full respect to such a Sadhu. Even if one member of the family disrespects a saint, the entire family suffers. Just like when Ravan insulted Vibhishan and kicked him, the entire country had to bear the brunt of the misdeed.

The second word is Sudha, which means elixir that removes 'Vish' (poison) and Visham Paristhiti (difficult situations and obstacles that we face).

Surtaru, or Kalpataru, is a wish-fulfilling tree which helps us get all that we desire.

Suman are beautiful flowers which bring a gift of beauty, joy, and fragrance.

Suphal are delicious and juicy fruits.

Suhavani Baat is good speech or piece of writing or even a good thought.

The last term of the verse, 'Tulsi Sita Pati Bhakti', indicates that devotion sprouts in our heart, which is the most propitious.

Thus, if you meet a Sadhu, you obtain all the terms that follow the word Sadhu in Goswami Tulsidas' couplet. In reality, it is a Sadhu who is the true Suphal (fruit) of our lives.

Are You A Visheyi, Sadhak Or Siddha-Find Out!

There are four stages that a disciple goes through to reach unalloyed purity and deep devotion towards his Guru.

The disciple–Guru relationship is said to be eternal and enduring. But even here, there are different categories of disciples or stages that a pupil goes through before reaching a purified sublime. Speaking on this topic on Day 54 of Hari Katha, famous Ramayana exponent Morari Bapu explained the rungs of a student's progression. A Guru, he said, is like a gardener who nurtures and protects learners without imposing the feeling of ownership on them. Yet, he carefully oversees their evolution on the spiritual path.

The main prerequisite is that the follower must have devotion and keen desire to learn rather than wanting to test his Master. Like during the war in Kurukshetra in Mahabharata, when Arjun became unsteady and was overcome by a sense of delusion, he took refuge in Lord Krishna. Total surrender at the feet of your Guru is essential to make progress.

In the second canto of the Guru Gita, Veda Vyasa writes:

"Kimatram bahnokten shastra koti shatairapi, durlabha chit vishrantihi vina guru kripa param."

Loosely translated it means that a person may study a thousand sacred texts, but his mind does not achieve peace without the grace of a Guru.

Morari Bapu said that the cleansing of the mind, its serenity and feeling of joy, cannot be achieved without the grace of a realized Guru. He added that a true Master does not rest till he has elevated his follower to the highest level.

But not all students are alike and there are categories depending on their qualities. In the Ram Charita Manas by Goswami Tulsidas, three classes of humans are mentioned.

Vishai sadhak siddh sayane, tribhid jeev jag bed bakhane

Ram sneh saras mun jasu, sadhu sabha bad aadar taasu

(According to the Vedas there are three types of embodied souls (human beings) in the world-the sensual, the seeker and the wise, who have attained perfection (in the form of God Realization). Of all these, he alone is highly honoured in an assembly of holy men, whose heart is full of love for Sri Ram.)

II Ram Charita Manas, Ayodhya Kaand-277.2 II

Bapu examined the categories individually:

Vishai: The majority belong to this group. Such a disciple cares for his wishes more than that of his Guru. Like a businessman who does a deal for his goods at his rate. Similarly, if our wishes are being fulfilled then we are happy, otherwise not. This attitude is a loss-making proposition as that student can't experience a Guru's grace. Mostly, people are full of desires and driven by them. If not fulfilled, a student can sometimes leave a Guru and also go to the extent of criticizing him.

Sadhak: A Sadhak is one '*Jo kabhi bhi kisi ke jeevan me badhak na bane*'–meaning one who never creates an impediment for another through thought, speech, or action. Such a person comes with his desires and wants them fulfilled, but alongside he keeps in mind what his Guru wishes.

The spiritual leader said that when we read the word Sadhak in reverse, it is K + Dha + Sa. This can be interpreted as "*Kalyankari dharam me jo nirantar savdhan rahta ho*", i.e., one who is constantly engaged and alert in dharma of welfare.

Siddha: He who does not forward his wishes but remains joyous in whatever his Master wishes. Like Bharat says in the Ramayana: "*Jeh bidhi prabhu prasanna mun hoi* (do as delights your heart, Lord Ram!)". The disciple understands that what he might be desiring might be a mistake and not in his welfare. So, he leaves all outcomes in the hands of his Guru and treats all events in his life as per the wishes of his Guru. Such a stand is full of benefits as a disciple's faith is in one alone and it becomes more and more unshakeable.

On the other hand, a disciple who after surrendering at the feet of one Guru then moves on to another Guru, brings pain to his original Master.

Besides these categories of students mentioned in the Ramayana, there is one student who is above all these categories, according to Morari Bapu. Such a student can be categorized as 'Shuddha'. Such a student feels that his Guru's wishes are like 'Hari Iccha'–God's will. Such a student doesn't only think that all outcomes in his life are due to his Guru's wishes but treats them as his *Param Kripa* i.e., Guru's supreme grace on him. He is constantly thinking about how his Guru, despite his supremely elevated state, due to his compassion is thinking about his disciple's welfare and that of the world.

To experience supreme grace, each student travels through these various stages before he achieves the state of unalloyed purity and devotion.

Jaun Kahan Taji Charan Tumhare-Tulsidas' Beautiful Entreaty To Lord Ram

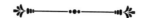

*R*efuge must be taken of one who is capable of giving it. Goswami Tulsidas in his poem explores the world around him and finds that only Lord Ram is able and compassionate enough to give him shelter.

Vinay Patrika is one of the most famous books of the Bhakti movement saint Goswami Tulsidas. This 16th century work contains a series of poems addressed to the main protagonists of the Ramayana like Lord Ram, Sita, Bharat, Lakshman, and Shatrughan, imploring them to free him from the evils of Kalayuga. On Day 55 of Hari Katha, illustrious Ramayana exponent Morari Bapu picked the 101st stanza of the book and explained it at length.

Jaun Kahan Taji Charan Tumhare,

Kako Naam Patit Paavan Jag, Kehi Ati Deen Piyare

Kaune Dev Barai Birad Hit, Hathi Hathi Adham Udhare

Khag, Mrig, Byadh, Paashan, Bitap Jad, Yavan Kavan Sur Tare

Dev, Danuj, Muni, Naag, Manuj Sab, Maya Bibas Bichare

Tinke Haath Das Tulsi Prabhu, Kaha Apanpau Haare

Jaun Kahan Taji Charan Tumhare

According to Morari Bapu, this stanza gives direction on all three paths–Bhakti (devotion), Gyana (knowledge) and Karma. In the poem, Goswami Tulsidas beseeches Lord Ram– "Where should I go leaving the refuge of your lotus feet?"

Jaun Kahan Taji Charan Tumhare,

Kako Naam Patit Paavan Jag, Kehi Ati Deen Piyare

Morari Bapu explained that Goswami Tulsidas knows that feet are meant for movement and will go away. Then why is he wanting to take refuge in them? Bapu clarified that just like when Krishna left for Mathura to complete his work as an avatar, he never actually left Vrindavan. Similarly, Lord Ram too never left Chitrakoot in reality. It is believed that these pilgrim centres are still full of divine consciousness. Therefore, Tulsidas knows that his place for refuge is permanent.

The next thought is–who is 'Patit Paavan' like Lord Ram? 'Patit Paavan' means a holy person who re-establishes the fallen. Bapu explained that all avatars come for a special purpose. Amongst all avatars, if there is one person who has been called *'Patit Paavan'*, it is Ram. Those like Tadaka, Subahu, Marich, Ahalya, Khar, Dushan, Kumbhakaran, Indrajeet and Ravan, all were sought out by Lord Ram and either re-established in Dharma or given Nirvana. For example, Ahalya had sung "Mai nari apavan, prabh jag paavan..." (I am an impure woman, while the Lord is able to sanctify the whole world), bringing out this sentiment beautifully.

In Lord Ram's entire journey, Morari Bapu counted that the prince of Ayodhya uplifted at least 14 main personalities.

Thus, Tulsi asks, "*Kehi ati deen pyare...*" (Who else loves those who are meek and downtrodden?)

Kaune Dev Barai Birad Hit, Hathi Hathi Adham Udhare

Khag, Mrig, Byadh, Paashan, Bitap Jad, Yavan Kavan Sur Tare

Goswami Tulsidas says not only does he elevate the sunk or destitute, but Lord Ram is also resolute in his will to do so. Whether it is birds, deer, hunters, trees or inanimate objects, there is none other like Lord Ram, who showers grace on all perforce. Tulsi refers to Jatayu, monkeys, bears, Ahalya who had turned into stone, trees like Yamla Arjun, Guh Nishad and Shabari, a lower caste tribal woman, all became subject of Lord Ram's love and blessings.

Dev, Danuj, Muni, Naag, Manuj Sab, Maya Bibas Bichare

Tinke Haath Das Tulsi Prabhu, Kaha Apanpau Haare

In these lines Tulsidas says that not just demons, snakes, or humans but even demigods are helpless. Morari Bapu said that there is a belief that a husband who is constrained by a dominating wife, citizens in the hands of a violent king, a son in the hands of an immoral father and simple people misled by a fundamentalist religious leader are all powerless and vulnerable.

Similarly, the demons were outwitted by demigods during the Samudra Manthan and foxed out of their fair share. When even sages like Shringi, Vishwamitra, Narad, Parashar can become deluded at some point, what can be said of humans who are always slave to Maya (illusion)!

Goswami Tulsidas says-how will such people who are themselves in bondage help me? Therefore, he has turned to Lord Ram who is fearless and adept in every way to salvage him.

Five Ways Of Gaining Spiritual Knowledge

*T*he drive for eternal truth has led many to search for sources of gaining knowledge. From where can we acquire this wisdom and how do we remain fixed in that knowledge?

The thirst of higher knowledge over and above the materialistic world has led many greats, like Buddha, to abandon their homes to find the ultimate truth. To unravel the layers of illusion around them and come in touch with their inner selves, to find out the real purpose of life. On achieving enlightenment many of these extraordinary personalities returned to spread the word among the ordinary people.

But spiritual knowledge can be obtained in myriad ways. Speaking on Day 56 of Hari Katha on the topic of where and how to seek this wisdom, Morari Bapu, enlisted at least five such methods.

1. Gurumukhi Gyana: The foremost way is from a Guru's mouth. This is the Vedic tradition where a disciple gains knowledge from the words and addresses of his Guru.

2. Suryamukhi Gyana: It is said that we can learn from the Sun. In the Upanishads, knowledge has been called 'Prakash' i.e., light. In the Brihadaranyaka Upanishad

there is a hymn about a prayer for us to move from darkness to light–'Tamso Ma Jyotirgamaya'. In our sacred epics, Lord Hanuman too acquired knowledge from his teacher Suryadeva.

3. Sanmukhi Gyana: When we sit in a holy congregation or in an ashram, we normally sit in front of a Guru and receive knowledge. Even if he doesn't speak like in the case of Dakshinamurthy Bhagavan, ignorance of disciples is dispelled and doubts cleared though his pure silence, merely by sitting quietly in front of him.

    In the Ramayana, there are scenes depicted of very old birds surrounding Kag Bhusundi to hear his ambrosial words. In this case, the Guru is young and students are old, but they are all sitting on the Nilgiri mountain facing Bhusundi to listen to Katha.

4. Munmukhi Gyana: In this case, knowledge is received through interpretation. A Guru says a few words and the student takes out meanings as per his mind and understanding. The risk here is that one may receive knowledge but not wisdom. This is more like a mind of a person becoming a library of information. But real wisdom is rarely gained in such a case.

5. Vedmukhi Gyana: This knowledge can be gained through the first three methods mentioned–Gurumukhi, Suryamukhi and Sanmukhi but also through the self-study of Vedas or scriptures.

Over and above, Bapu quoted the Ram Charita Manas which says, *'Binu Guru hoi ki gyan, gyan ki hoi birag binu'* (Uttar Kaand-Soratha-89.1)–Can knowledge ever be obtained without a

Guru? And can one stay fixed in that knowledge without having reached a state of detachment?

In Yog Vashishth, it is written that spiritual knowledge can only be obtained by being a Gurumukh i.e., a true follower of your Master. The scripture further says that Vairagya or detachment that comes due to some event or occurrence in one's life is not real but temporary. However, dispassion that emerges from Vivek (mental discretion) is true and permanent.

13 Questions That Will Change Your Life

Query holds a central place in spiritual development. It directs the seeker to find higher and subtler meanings in life.

Most spiritual journeys start with a question. When the world around us does not satisfy us, self-enquiry begins. Ramana Maharishi famously exhorted all those who came to him to seek the answer to the question, "Who Am I?" But this might be difficult for us, as we usually need a guide. Thus, queries to a Master hold an important place.

What is Satvik and Tatvik Jigyasa?

Speaking on Day 57 of Hari Katha, spiritual light Morari Bapu made a distinction between Satvik and Tatvik Jigyasa (pure or moral enquiry versus elemental enquiry). He said that 'Satvik' dialogue is one that doesn't have even a hint of Rajo Guna (anything done in the Mode of Passion). The idea should not be to impress others or win their praise and applause. 'Satvik' dialogue begins and ends in the mode of peace and in the middle one finds the answers.

'Tatvik' dialogue is one where there is discussion on the subtlest of elements of matter. For example, the act of washing requires soap, water, and effort to clean. Soap is like Gyana (knowledge), effort is Karma and water is like Bhakti or devotion.

What is Moksha?

Bapu also elaborated to say that our soul itself is our Buddhpurush (realized soul). And that the contemporary definition of Moksha (salvation) should be done as Mo = Moh and Ksh + Shay-in whose life all delusion has been completely destroyed. Bapu said this is especially pertinent as one is constantly searching for salvation after death, without even learning to live life fully. We need to first remove delusion from our present lives. He advised that an aspirant needed to stay away from unnecessary controversies to achieve Moksha through self-improvement.

Giving another dimension to the conversation, Morari Bapu added that there are three vices of Dambh (pretense), Kapat (shrewdness or guile) to hide our faults of anger and lust, and Ahankar (ego). To be able to get rid of these three can also be construed as achieving salvation. Besides, one should also stay away from Ninda (criticism), Irsha (envy), and Dwesh (hatred). Bapu then went on to deliver crisp remedies to the most complex of questions posed to him.

Which is the biggest Daan (donation): When we are on the side of truth, and also capable, yet we forgive the person who has wronged us.

Which is the biggest Tap (penance): To free oneself of all desires.

What is the biggest Shaurya (act of valour): To win over one's own Swabhav (innate nature).

Which is the biggest Gyana/Satya (true knowledge): To see God or good in the whole world. To remain positive in our outlook of everything and see the best qualities and traits in everyone around us.

Which is the best Season: Sweet truth in our speech.

Which is the best Sanyasa (ascetism): Tyaag (sacrifice).

Which is the best Wealth: Living by Dharma or moral code.

What is Dharma (moral code): Truth, Love, Compassion.

Which is biggest Yagna (sacrificial fire): God himself–we put everything in the sacrificial fire as an offering to God. In the act of doing a yagna, there is primacy on doing 'Swaha Swaha' (offering and giving up) rather than 'Wah Wah' (seeking self-praise). Else, learned men have espoused that 'Hari Naam' (chanting of God's name) can be considered to be the biggest Yagna.

Which is biggest Dakshina (spiritual gift): Gyana Updesha (deliverance of knowledge).

Which is the biggest Strength: Pranayama i.e., control of our breath. This is also awareness and regulation of our breath.

What Should Be The Qualities Of A Devotee And A True Guru?

*L*istening is an art and more so when it is about a devotee listening to a discourse to obtain spiritual knowledge and to understand the mysteries of life and death. The main condition is that the Guru must also be fully accomplished.

The famous expounder of the Ramayana, Morari Bapu, started Day 58 of Hari Katha on a personal note. Famous for taking Goswami Tulsidas' Ram Charita Manas to the hearts and homes of millions of people, Bapu paid ode to his Guru and grandfather Tribhuvana Das ji. While Bapu is considered one of the greatest authorities of Ram Katha, he said that it was his constant experience that only his lips move and that words flow by the inspiration of his Guru. In one sense, he is also a Shrota (listener) of the discourse that he is delivering.

Bapu elaborated that a Vakta i.e., the person delivering a sermon, should never have a sense of superiority that the listener is ignorant. A realized soul always gives respect to everyone, as he understands that all beings are capable of enlightenment; only the curtain of illusion needs to be lifted. The eyes, words, and the pure touch of a Buddhpurush (realized soul) have the capacity to remove this curtain.

Ram Katha, the narration of the story of Ram, is deep. Finding the right 'Patra' (eligible recipient) is also important, as illustrated in Lord Shiva's discussion with his consort Parvati.

Shrota Sumati Sushila Suchi Katha Rasika Hari Dasa,

Pai Uma Ati Gopyamapi Sajjana Karahiu Prakasa

II Ram Charita Manas–Uttar Kaand–Doha 69B II

This means the listener of the narration should be:

1. Sumati: A person with the right thinking

2. Sushil: Good natured and virtuous

3. Suchi: Pious or pure from inside and outside

4. Katha Rasik: Should be deeply interested in the narration

5. Hari Das: A devotee of Shri Hari / God

Saints reveal their profoundest secrets upon finding such a deserving recipient of spiritual knowledge.

Examining the Shrotas in Ram Charita Manas, Morari Bapu said the first is Tulsi's own Mun (mind). Goswami Tulsidas says that Ram Katha was narrated by his Guru to him repeatedly, and only after a long time was he able to absorb it and put it into words. Bapu advised that even if one takes a long time to comprehend, the listener should fully assimilate the principal points.

The second Shrota of Ramayana is Bharadwaj Muni, who listens to Katha at the feet of an accomplished sage like Yagnavalika. Third is Parvati, who is listening under a banyan tree on the peak of Kailash to her husband Shiva. And lastly is Garuda, who is sitting with the fully realized soul, Bhusundi, on the Nilgiri mountain.

Other great listeners in our scriptures include Arjun, who listened to Lord Krishna in the middle of the battleground of Kurukshetra in Mahabharata. Symbolically, Krishna is the charioteer and Arjun is the rider, just like the person delivering a sermon must be the guide for the listener.

As far as Sankhya Yoga is concerned, son Kapil preaches to mother, Devahuti, and in the Bhagavata Purana, Parikshit listened to Shukdeva.

In the Mahabharata, Vidur was asked the qualities one needs to possess to reach heaven. As per the maxims of 'Vidur Niti', there are two types of people who can achieve heaven. Firstly, one who is fully capable of dispensing punishment and yet forgives the person who has wronged him. Secondly, the person who himself is a man of small means and yet has the mentality of sharing with others.

Morari Bapu explained that a Sadhu or an enlightened person, when he speaks, he too is sharing and making enormous endowments on the listener by giving the following:

Gyana Daan: The gift of knowledge

Vidya Daan: The gift of learning

Vardaan: A boon

Dhanyavaad: The gift of gratitude

Abhay Daan: The gift of fearlessness

Kshama Daan: The gift of forgiveness

Prem Daan: The gift of love, which is the supreme gift

Spiritual guide Morari Bapu then went on to narrate the story of Nachiketa in Kathoupanishada and shared the thoughts of Tadrupanand Maharaj of Manan Ashram about an able seeker and listener or a devotee and a Guru.

1. A listener should be like Nachiketa and the deliverer of the sermon should be like Yamacharya.

2. A listener should have deep regard for his mother, father and have devotion while the speaker should be polite and knowledgeable.

3. Nachiketa waited for three days for Yamaraj without food or water–waiting for the teacher. Here hunger and thirst should be interpreted as desire in a devotee for learning and to obtain knowledge. In turn, the Master should give the devotee respect and regard as Yamaraj gives to Nachiketa. The Guru should be willing to share his knowledge.

4. A listener should be Satya Nishta (rooted in truth) and have faith that his Master will always speak the truth. Even if a devotee cannot always be honest, at least he must have faith that his Guru is always truthful.

5. A listener should have desire for discretion and detachment and firm faith that he will get these from the place where he has taken refuge. And the Master should indeed bestow these qualities upon him.

6. A devotee should be sharp in mind and intellect and easily accepting of knowledge being given to him. He should not doubt, nor should his mind be scattered. His Guru must know the mysteries of life and death.

7. A devotee should not desire heaven and its associated pleasures but want spiritual knowledge and the Guru should be a repository of knowledge, devotion, detachment, and dispassion.

And while listening is such an art, as described above, a devotee must absorb everything from his Guru, not just his words. Morari Bapu advocated that a student must observe his Master and try and understand his silence, learn from his eyes, his gestures, and even his tears.

Comparing And Contrasting Sita And Draupadi

*S*ita and Draupadi are two of the most charismatic women protagonists from the Hindu epics. While one is calm like a still river on a full moon night, the other encompasses the passion of a roaring blaze.

There is a physical fire and a spiritual fire. Satsanga, or attending holy congregations, is one method by which our internal fire is ignited. "So yagna can be a physical yagna like the one that is invoked for rituals; another is 'Maun Yagna', a silent yagna like the one between Adi Shankaracharya and his disciples, where pupils learn from his silence. Illustrious exponent of the Ramayana, Morari Bapu explained that another is 'Mukhar Satsanga', where words are used. Then, there is a discussion where a free flow of thoughts is allowed even from devotees–that is called 'Mukta Satsanga'.

Staying on the topic of yagna, Morari Bapu went on to speak about Draupadi on Day 59 of Hari Katha, saying she was born out of the holy fire. He then compared her to Sita, who was a blessing from the earth's womb. Drawing similarities and distinctions, he enlisted several points for these two feminine personalities, who are central to Hindu epics and beliefs.

The spiritual leader explained that Sita is a fair maiden and thus called 'Shweta' whereas Draupadi has a wheatish hue and thus called 'Krsna'. One belonged to the Treta Yuga while the other appeared in Dwapara Yuga. In terms of disposition, Sita is calm while Draupadi is fiery. Sita has fortitude, Draupadi is hot blooded. Both have Swayamvar, an event organized to choose the groom, in which many kings participate. In Sita's Swayamvar, Narayan i.e. Ram comes and wins her hand, while in the case of Draupadi, Nar i.e. Arjun emerges victorious.

During the Swayamvar, Ram looks up towards the gallery where Sita is sitting with her friends and is highly agitated about the outcome. The condition to win her hand was that Ram needed to break Lord Shiva's bow. To win Draupadi, Arjun looks into the water to catch a reflection of the fish-eye that he needs to pierce with an arrow. Bapu interpreted the breaking of the bow to discarding the idea of war while piercing a target as symbolic of battle.

Ram attends the event as a prince of Ayodhya, so he is revealed and lauded while Arjun is in hiding and comes in the garb of a Brahmin. Eventually, Ram and Sita unite in matrimony but in Draupadi's case she needed to submit to five husbands.

In Janaki's Swayamvar, Lord Shiva is in imperceptible form of the bow and Sita prays to him to help make the weapon light; in Draupadi's Swayamvar, Krishna is physically present.

Sita's eyes have tears (in this context water) of fear and hope, and a simile is drawn by Goswami Tulsidas with a fish, while in Draupadi's case a fish is hung over water in a pond.

Sita was born from earth and eventually returned to it, while Draupadi appeared from fire and disappeared into the icy Himalayas. In one sense, eventually at the end of their lives, Sita returns to the lap of earth while Draupadi rises above into the Himalayas. Ironically, Sita was fair and disappeared into brownish earth while Draupadi was wheatish and disappeared into the white snow.

Ravan abducts Sita while Dushasan attempts to disrobe Draupadi. The abduction of Sita takes place in solitude while Draupadi's disrobing happens in public. When Sita was being abducted, Giddharaj Jattayu comes to her aid, while Vikaran stands up against the injustice meted out to Draupadi.

In Sita's case, her father Janak had taken a vow on the condition of her marriage while Draupadi took a vow to avenge her insult.

Sita went into a 14-year exile while Draupadi was banished with her husbands for 12 years, with an additional year that was to be spent in hiding. Sita went through trial by fire to prove her chastity during 'Agnipariksha', after she was rescued from Ravan, Draupadi herself is fire personified as she had emerged from sacrificial fire. During her time apart from Lord Ram, Sita's body emaciates, and her hair hangs like a string while Draupadi let her hair loose after her attempted disrobing.

In the Ramayana, Ravan is called a dog as he wears the attire of a Sadhu but indulges in crime; Draupadi is accompanied by dog in her final days, and it is said that the dog symbolized Dharma.

The similarities and contrasts are endless, but each of the two figures was great in her own right.

The Art Of Making Our Daily Karma A Yagna

What should our actions be led by? What should our intention be at the start of each endeavour, and how should we bear its outcome?

Can a human being stay without doing karma even for a moment? This was a question that was taken up at the beginning of Day 60 of Hari Katha by spiritual luminary, Morari Bapu. Answering the same, he said that no one can stay without doing something or the other, even for a fraction of a moment. Even if it is our eyes moving, or fingers snapping, or our ears listening to myriad sounds, we are always engaged in some action. If all of this were to come to a perfectly motionless state, our Mun (mind) would not sit still even for a minute.

Question from a listener: Who is a Sadhu?

Morari Bapu: There is a Sanskrit Shloka (verse):

Satyamev Vrataṁ Yasya Dayā Dineṣu Sarvadā.

Kāmakrodhau Vaśe Yasya Sa Sādhuḥ- Kathyate Budhaiḥ

(Only one who has a vow of truth, who always serves the poor, who is in control of lust and anger, he is called a "Sadhu" by the wise.)

Elaborating on the meaning of this, Morari Bapu enlisted the characteristics of a Sadhu:

1. A Sadhu dwells in truth-in his thoughts, words, and deeds.

2. Is constantly bestowing compassion on the poor and the marginalized.

3. Can control lust and anger, not through force but through understanding.

Compassion is the natural disposition of a Sadhu. Compassion is not a deed for him, but his nature. He is a person who has achieved 'Swaroop Bodh', which means self-enlightenment. He becomes 'Akarta'-a person who does without doing. He does not have a sense of ego or self in the actions that he does. Rather, actions happen on their own.

Even in the Bhagvad Gita, Lord Krishna advocates to Arjun to undertake Karma that come naturally-'Sahajam Karma Kauntayaha'. This advice comes in the Gita after an elaborate explanation on the three types of Karma-Satvik (mode of goodness), Rajsik (mode of passion), Tamsik (mode of ignorance).

Krishna calls unattached actions as Karma yoga, where a person is adept, in all that he does but remains untouched by his actions or its fruits. Just like Krishna is highly skilled in the large canvass of work that he accomplished in his lifetime, yet he remains 'Akarta'-the non-doer.

Question: Should there be contentment in Bhajan (constant remembrance of the Divine and praying) or should we have a desire to keep doing more and more?

Morari Bapu: Contentment in Bhajan is like death. Bhajan should become our breath, as natural as that to our being. Not everything is understood through reading and writing—that what is left in terms of understanding is comprehended through Bhajan.

Question: How can we make our Karma into a yoga? How can we make our Karma into a yagna?

Morari Bapu: If we follow the following principles, our work will become a yagna. Each Karma of ours can become a yagna:

1. If we do all our actions leaving 'Ahamta' and 'Mamata' i.e., without ego or attachment. Our thinking should be that I am not doing this work for myself but for the universe. Like the physical yagna that one does, the person adds ghee, jawar, etc. but the flames and scent that emerge belong to all, not just the person doing the yagna.

2. Never do any Karma in Spardha (competition) but with Shraddha (devotion). If we do our work with a sense of devotion, we rise above petty sense of winning or losing. Like a person playing a game can win but the sense should not be of Jai (defeating someone) but Vijay (sense of achievement). In Vijay, there is no sense of superiority derived out of trouncing another. Vijay is achieved by doing Karma through devotion. We should also follow these simple rules:

    a. Do all Karma with Niti—in a righteous way.

b. Do all Karma with right Riti–using correct method.

c. Do all Karma with Priti–with love.

3. Do all Karma as Nimit–considering yourself a mere instrument of a superior power.

4. Never do Karma for 'Badla'(revenge) but as 'Balidaan'(sacrifice), which means we should never undertake an action to seek revenge but always with a sacrificial intention.

5. Asakti Mukt Karma–there should be no attachment or infatuation about the outcome. The thinking should be that if what we wish happens, well and good; if it doesn't happen, don't worry about it.

6. Taking the above point forward, don't do your actions for 'Phal' but for 'Ras'–not for the fruit but the juice (here juice means the joy of doing something). The enjoyment of doing the action is more important than its outcome. If we do work with this temperament, then the universe starts aiding our efforts.

7. Never show off–However glamorous the action and outcome, we should never have vanity. We should never be pretentious.

8. If the outcome is adverse, have the mentality that you will bear it yourself. If the outcome is auspicious, share it with others.

These are not words of lofty spiritualism but apply to our day to day lives; form the art of living.

Dealing With Sorrow-
Buddha And Beyond

*I*f there is sorrow in this world, we must examine its causes. But also remember and celebrate all that is joyous in our lives.

On the final day of Hari Katha (Day 61), Morari Bapu began with a discussion on Gautama Buddha. He said that Buddha has spoken about Four Noble Truths:

1. There is suffering and sorrow in the world

2. There are causes or reasons for the sorrow

3. There are solutions to end our grief

4. The path that leads to cessation of sorrow also helps us reach Samadhi (Deep trance)

Bapu then explained that, first of all, birth itself brings pain. Not only does the mother experience great physical agony during delivery of a child, but the baby too suffers and cries as he emerges from the womb.

Death is also a cause sorrow. The person who dies undergoes pain, and there are several reasons for that. Death opens a barrage of questions that the person helplessly stares at: what would happen to his soul, what will happen of the dear and loved ones left behind, and the like. Even physically, a person experiences pain as the soul separates itself from the body.

Old age is sorrow as witnessed by Buddha when he went for a chariot ride in his kingdom. Disease also brings distress.

What are the principal reasons that cause us to suffer is the next question. The root of the answer lies in Trishna–endless desires.

It is said that Trishna means Tri + Eshana which means three types of desires. These are:

1. Suteshana–desire for offspring
2. Vitteshsna–desire for wealth
3. Lokeshana–desire for fame / to be lauded by society

Gautama Buddha feels that these three are the root cause of all suffering. After exploring the nature and causes of sorrow, he pronounced the 8-fold path which helps humans in finding a balance, the middle way.

The moot idea is that Trishna should either get destroyed or become balanced. At least we should not have extreme level of desire for anything.

However, Bapu also added a personal perspective to the teachings of Buddha. Rather than seeing the darker side of life and examining sorrow, one could also evaluate existence in the light of positivity. We should think:

1. If there is sorrow, there is also happiness

2. If a life well–lived is a source of joy, then saints also celebrate death. In Vaishnav Sadhus, Samadhi is also treated as a celebration.

3. If youth is joy, old age should also be viewed as a source of happiness as elders are respected and cared for.

4. Illness is sorrow but we should also acknowledge that due to disease our negative Karmas or imbalanced living get neutralised. We also develop inner strength and develop a mentality of accepting things which itself eases pain. Disease should be viewed as a penance. It purifies us.

Just like Buddha searched for causes of sorrow, we can also explore the reasons for joy and there are many.

1. As souls we are Anand Swaroop–bliss is our intrinsic nature.

2. Meeting with saints is a cause of joy in our life as is meeting with good people.

3. Hope in life is a reason for happiness.

4. Our good deeds should make us happy.

5. And ultimately, the remembrance of God brings peace and bliss.